C000173062

D

Your Step-by-Step Guide
to Building Welsh Sentences

D.I.Y. WELSH

Your Step-by-Step Guide
to Building Welsh Sentences.

*Sut i Adeiladu Brawddegau Cymraeg –
Gam wrth Gam*

D. GERAINT LEWIS

Gomer

First published in 2018 by
Gomer Press, Llandysul, Ceredigion SA44 4JL
www.gomer.co.uk

Reprinted: 2019

ISBN 978 1 78562 215 1

This book is published with the financial support of the
Welsh Books Council.

Printed and bound in Wales by
Gomer Press, Llandysul, Ceredigion.

Foreword

This little book is intended for those of you who may have difficulty with traditional grammar. It's based on the patterns found in formal, written Welsh – which are far fewer than the variety of forms found in the spoken language.

Welsh doesn't work in the same way as English and the major continental languages. So, when exploring new territory, take your time and pay attention to each step. Be patient and accept that learning something completely new is going to take some time and effort.

- Work your way through the exercises, enjoy the different approach, celebrate each step forward:
  - be prepared to go back if you are unsure, and
  - don't move on until you are happy that you understand what you are doing.
- Take note of the boxes marked \|/ (the druidic symbol for knowledge and wisdom).
- Take pride in what you have achieved when you move on.

You will find that Welsh is <u>not</u> more difficult than any other language; it's just **different**.

I wish to record here my gratitude to: Father Stephen Edwards and Llinos Dafis for their encouragement; Gwasg Gomer for continuing to produce my books to the highest standards; and especially to my friend, Susan Jenkins, who has helped to knock this text into shape. However, any errors remaining are mine alone.

D. Geraint Lewis
Llangwyryfon
February 2018

5

Introduction

DIY Welsh makes use of a system of coloured 'building blocks' to show you how to write correct Welsh.

---

nouns (the names of things) are either **pink** or **blue**

adjectives (words that describe things) are **orange**

verb-nouns (the names of actions) are **green**

This little book is based on the structures and spelling of formal, written Welsh. There is far more variety in the spoken language, but the mutations, for example, occur in both forms of Welsh. My intention here is to provide you with an understanding of the basic components of Welsh as a base from which to move on to acquiring the variations that occur in the spoken language.

The book is divided into five sections.

Part 1: A Dictionary in Pink and Blue

This deals with Welsh **nouns, adjectives** and the **soft mutation**. In this respect, Welsh has two important characteristics:

1. All singular nouns in Welsh are either **masculine** or **feminine**. Please note that these categories relate to the noun's grammatical 'gender' (like 'le' or 'la' in French), not to its 'sex'.
2. Certain letters at the beginning of a word can 'mutate' or change. This section deals with the most common of these mutations: the **Treiglad Meddal** (the 'Soft' mutation).

Part 1 also includes:

- A short list of Welsh nouns (enwau), together with some common Emojis.
- An Exercise: 'Remember the gender'. At the end of the book there is an appendix with more suggestions on how to remember the gender.

Part 2: Describe and Do

This deals with Welsh **verb-nouns**. This section also includes:

- A list of common Welsh prepositions – *to, from, over, under,* etc.
- An Exercise: How to remember the prepositions that trigger mutation.
- A basic list of **verb-nouns** (the equivalent of the infinitive in English *to* do, *to* go, *to* describe, etc.) and mutatable **adjectives**. These lists can be used in conjunction with the list of nouns in Part 1 to create your own sentences.

Part 3: In the Workshop

This shows how the **Past tense** works in Welsh and describes the 'little words' – the nuts, bolts, springs and screws – that are used to connect words when building the Welsh sentence. It also includes some information about:

- Personal pronouns – *I, me, my,* etc.
- The other Welsh mutations.

Part 4: Numerals and Telling and Time

Part 5: Y Geiriadur – The Dictionary

A full-colour basic Welsh–English/English–Welsh Dictionary.

Appendix 1: The Little Words and the Mutations they trigger
Appendix 2: Remember the Gender

For:
The order of the Welsh alphabet see p. 86
A short list of **nouns** see p. 22
A short list of **adjectives** see p. 39
A short list of **verb-nouns** see p. 39
Prepositions see p. 37
The 'little words' that trigger mutation see p. 103
Numerals see p. 60
Telling the Time see p. 67
Pronouns see p. 53
Mutations see p. 57
English–Welsh Dictionary p. 71
Welsh–English Dictionary p. 86
Remember the Gender p. 109

Part 1

A Dictionary in Pink and Blue

In order to use this manual you need to learn about some basic grammatical features of Welsh.

1. Masculine and Feminine Nouns

Here are some of the basic grammatical features of Welsh:
eg (enw gwrywaidd/ *masculine noun*) **ci** *eg* a dog
eb (enw benywaidd/ *feminine noun*)   **cath** *eb* a cat

There is no indefinite article (a) in Welsh 'ci' = **a** dog; 'cath' = **a** cat

In speech and in print
a masculine noun may be followed by *hwn*:
'y ci *hwn*' (this dog)
and a feminine noun may be followed by *hon*:
'y gath *hon*' (this cat)

In this book

a feminine noun is printed in Pink	**cath** cat
a masculine noun is printed in Blue	**ci** dog

2. The Soft Mutation (Treiglad Meddal)

This affects the following letters:

C	P	T
G	B	D
Ll	M	Rh

3. Parts of Speech

For reasons that will become clear as you work your way through the exercises we shall use the Welsh terms:

noun – the name of a 'thing' **enw**
adjective – a describing word **ansoddair**
verb-noun – the name of an 'action' **berfenw**
mutation – the manner in which certain letters at the beginning of a word can change **treiglad**

Here's some information about these terms:

enw (plural **enwau**)
Every **enw** in Welsh is either masculine or feminine (this is its 'gender' and is not the same as 'sex'), e.g. *a girl* '**merch**' and *a cat* '**cath**' are **feminine**; *a boy* '**bachgen**' and *a dog* '**ci**' are **masculine**

ansoddair (plural **ansoddeiriau**)
The **ansoddair** usually <u>follows</u> the noun in Welsh, **ci** (enw) **du** (ansoddair) *a black* (adjective) *dog* (noun)

berfenw (plural **berfenwau**)
As in many other languages the **berfenw** can be conjugated – that is, its form changes according to whom is performing the action and when they are doing it.

treiglad (plural **treigladau**)
cath (*cat*) may appear as **g**ath **ch**ath **ngh**ath

4. The Welsh Alphabet

The Welsh alphabet is not the same as the English alphabet. It may look similar in places, but it also contains pairs of letters which signify a single letter sound in Welsh. You will come across three of these letter combinations when coming to terms with mutation:

dd as pronounced in *the* and *that*
ll (a letter not found in other European languages) put the tongue in the **l** position and 'hiss'. Watch some rugby and say **Llanelli**.
rh as in *perhaps* or when referring the the River *Rhine*.

(In Welsh alphabetical order the double letters follow the single letter. **Dd** follows **d**, **ll** follows **l**, and **rh** follows **r**. **See more about this on page 86 where you'll learn how to use a Welsh dictionary**.)

This book uses the colours shown above in a system of 'building blocks' which will help you to construct a Welsh sentence step by step.

An Exercise in Pink and Blue

If you're using Welsh you can't really avoid mutations. So we'll start with the most common mutation, **Treiglad Meddal** (Soft Mutation). Let's take it a step at a time.

Step 1

Learn the jingle:

C (see)	**P** (pee)	**T** (tee)
G (gee)	**B** (bee)	**D** (dee)
Ll (ell)	**M** (em)	**Rh** (rhee)

Soon you'll remember what letters are affected by **Treiglad Meddal**. Then you'll need to know what happens to them, and before too long you'll be merrily mutating. Using the **Treiglad Meddal** means that:

C	softens to	**G**
P	softens to	**B**
T	softens to	**D**
G	disappears completely	
B	softens to	**F**
D	softens to	**Dd**
Ll	softens to	**L**
M	softens to	**F**
Rh	softens to	**R**

Enw (noun)

The singular **enw** in Welsh is either **masculine** or **feminine**.

> a feminine **enw** is printed in **Pink**   **merch** *a girl*; **cath** *a cat*
> a masculine **enw** is printed in **Blue**   **bachgen** *a boy*; **ci** *a dog*

A good way to start using **Treiglad Meddal** is to add an **ansoddair** to an **enw**. Or as you'd say in English, add an adjective to a noun.

Step 2

When an **ansoddair** follows a **masculine** noun (**enw**), nothing changes and so we get combinations like:

ci coch (a red dog) and **ceffyl du** (a black horse)

However, when an **ansoddair** follows a **feminine** noun (**enw**), **Treiglad Meddal** takes place and we get examples like:

cath goch (a red cat) and **ceg fawr** (a big mouth)

Here you can see that **after** cath the 'c' softens to **g**, and after ceg the 'm' softens to **f**.

Don't mutate adjectives following plural nouns, even if those nouns are feminine. An adjective will only mutate if it follows a singular feminine noun.

In order to help you to practise using **Treiglad Meddal**, here's a selection of mutatable adjectives. You'll see that they all begin with one of the letters in the jingle at the beginning of Step 1.

C		**P**		**T**	
coch	*red*	**pert**	*pretty*	**tal**	*tall*
cas	*nasty*	**poeth**	*hot*	**tew**	*fat*
G		**B**		**D**	
glân	*clean*	**bach**	*little*	**da**	*good*
gwan	*weak*	**byr**	*short*	**drwg**	*bad*
Ll		**M**		**Rh**	
llawn	*full*	**mawr**	*big*	**rhad**	*cheap*
llwyd	*grey*	**melyn**	*yellow*	**rhyfedd**	*strange*

Work your way through the following simple exercises to become comfortable in the use of Treiglad Meddal, which occurs very frequently in Welsh. In order to complete the exercises, you will also need to use the list of nouns starting on page 22.

C softens to **G** following a feminine enw

- merch + cas (*nasty*) *becomes* _____
- bachgen + cas *becomes* _____
- cath + coch (*red*) *becomes* _____
- ci + coch *becomes* _____

Pick out random pink and blue words from the List on p. 22 followed by **coch** *and* **cas**

P softens to **B** following a feminine enw

- merch + poeth (*hot*) *becomes* _____
- bachgen + poeth *becomes* _____
- cath + pert (*pretty*) *becomes* _____
- ci + pert *becomes* _____

Pick out random pink and blue words from the List on p. 22 followed by **pert** and **poeth**

T softens to **D** following a feminine enw

- merch + tal (*tall*) *becomes* _____
- bachgen + tal *becomes* _____
- cath + tew (*fat*) *becomes* _____
- ci + tew *becomes* _____

Pick out random pink and blue words from the List on p. 22 followed by **tal** *and* **tew**

G disappears altogether following a feminine enw

- merch + gwan (*weak*) *becomes* _____
- bachgen + gwan *becomes* _____
- cath + glân (*clean*) *becomes* _____
- ci + glân *becomes* _____

Pick out random pink and blue words from the List on p. 22 followed by **gwan** *and* **glân**

B softens to **F** following a feminine enw
- merch + byr (*short*) *becomes* _____
- bachgen + byr *becomes* _____
- cath + bach (*little*) *becomes* _____
- ci + bach *becomes* _____

Pick out random pink and blue words from the List on p. 22 followed by **bach** *and* **byr**

D softens to **Dd** following a feminine enw
merch + da (*good*) *becomes* _____
bachgen + da *becomes* _____
cath + drwg (*bad*) *becomes* _____
ci + drwg *becomes* _____

Pick out random pink and blue words from the List on p. 22 followed by **da** *and* **drwg**

Ll softens to **L** following a feminine enw
- merch + llawn (*full*) *becomes* _____
- bachgen + llawn *becomes* _____
- cath + llwyd (*grey*) *becomes* _____
- ci + llwyd *becomes* _____

Pick out random pink and blue words from the List on p. 22 followed by **llawn** *and* **llwyd**

M softens to **F** following a feminine enw
- merch + mawr (*big*) *becomes* _____
- bachgen + mawr *becomes* _____
- cath + melyn (*yellow*) *becomes* _____
- ci + melyn *becomes* _____

Pick out random pink and blue words from the List on p. 22 followed by **mawr** *and* **melyn**

Rh softens to **R** following a feminine enw
- merch + rhyfedd (*strange*) *becomes* _____
- bachgen + rhyfedd *becomes* _____
- cath + rhad (*cheap*) *becomes* _____
- ci + rhad *becomes* _____

Pick out random pink and blue words from the List on p. 22 followed by **rhyfedd** *and* **rhad**

Step 3

The definite article ('the') has three forms in Welsh:
1. **y** = the
2. **yr** before a vowel – 'yr afal', and 'h' 'yr haul'
3. **'r** following a vowel – 'y ci a'r bachgen'

No mutation occurs when **'y'** appears before a masculine **enw**
   y + bachgen = **y** bachgen
   y + ci = **y** ci

However, **Treiglad Meddal** is (almost always) triggered when **'y'** appears before a feminine enw. See \l/ for the exceptions.

   y + merch = **y** ferch
   y + cath = **y** gath

> \l/
> The letters **'ll'** and **'rh'** do not mutate after **'y'**, e.g. *y llaw, y rhaw*, although these nouns are feminine.

Practise your new knowledge by doing the following exercises.

C
- y + cadair *chair*   = _____
- y + ceffyl *horse*   = _____
- y + cannwyll *candle* = _____

Put 'y' before other pink and blue words starting with **C** from the List on p. 22

P
- y + pêl *ball*   = _____
- y + parti *party*   = _____
- y + pont *bridge*   = _____

Put 'y' before other pink and blue words starting with **P** from the List on p. 22

T
- y + telyn *harp*   = _____
- y + to *roof*   = _____
- y + troed *foot*   = _____

Put 'y' before other pink and blue words starting with **T** from the List on p. 22

G *when 'G' disappears and leaves a vowel,* **y** *becomes* **yr** *before a vowel*
- y + gardd *garden* = _____
- y + gwallt *hair*   = _____
- y + gafr *goat*   = _____

Put 'y' before other pink and blue words starting with **G** from the List on p. 22

B
- y + basged *basket* = _____
- y + bachgen *boy*   = _____
- y + buwch *cow*   = _____

Put 'y' before other pink and blue words starting with **B** from the List on p. 22

D

- y + dafad *sheep* = _____
- y + drws *door* = _____
- y + draig *dragon* = _____

Put 'y' before other pink and blue words starting with **D** from the List on p. 22

M

- y + mam *mother* = _____
- y + mochyn *pig* = _____
- y + modrwy *ring* = _____

Put 'y' before other pink and blue words starting with **M** from the List on p. 22

Remember the exceptions!

> \|/
> '**ll**' and '**rh**'
> **ansoddair** mutates
> **enw** does not

Ll

- y + lleuad *moon* = _____
- y + llew *lion* = _____
- y + llaw *hand* = _____

Put 'y' before other pink and blue words starting with **Ll** from the List on p. 22

Rh

- y + rhaff *rope* = _____
- y + rhosyn *rose* = _____
- y + rhaw *shovel* = _____

Put 'y' before other pink and blue words starting with **Rh** from the List on p. 22

Step 4

yr is the definite article which becomes **'r** <u>following</u> a vowel

a = *and,* **a** + **yr** = **a'r** (*and the*) 'y ci a'r bachgen'

Put together:
  y + cadair + du, **a'r** + pêl + coch, **a'r** + telyn + tal, **a'r** + gwiwer + pert, **a'r** + llong + llwyd, **a'r** + dafad + drwg

In no time at all you'll be able to complete a full sentence.

Step 5

All you need to do is put '**Mae**' at the beginning of the list and '**yn**' at the end followed by a **verb-noun (berfenw)**.

Mae'r bachgen bach a'r ferch fawr yn chwarae (to play)
(The little boy and the big girl are playing.)

This is your basic Welsh sentence with all mutations correct and in place.

Now it's over to you to complete the following sentences!

Mae'r + merch + bach a'r + bachgen + drwg a'r + ci + du a'r + cath + brown **yn** + (a verb-noun) **cerdded** *(to walk).*

Mae'r aderyn + du a'r iâr + bach + coch **yn bwyta** *(to eat)* bwyd y + mochyn + tew.

Mae'r car + coch a'r fan + mawr + glas a'r lorri + llwyd **yn dilyn** *(to follow)* y + beic.

> 'Remember the Gender' on page 109 offers tips on how to remember whether a noun is masculine or feminine.

A Basic List of Welsh Nouns (enwau)

In order to find your way around this list, or indeed any Welsh dictionary, you need to understand the Welsh alphabet and, in particular, the 'double' letters given in bold type below.

The Welsh alphabet

a b c **ch** d **dd** e f **ff** g **ng** h i j l **ll** m n o p **ph** r **rh** s t **th** u w y

For an explanation of how this affects word order, go to page 86.

Note too that there is no indefinite article (a/an) in Welsh and so 'aderyn' means '**a** bird' and 'blodyn' means '**a** flower', etc.

This list includes:

1. The Welsh words for some common **Emojis**.
2. A list of coloured **Emojis** for you to name in Welsh.
3. A list of black **Emojis** for you to name in Welsh and state the colour.
4. Some other useful nouns.

a
aderyn (a) bird
afal (an) apple
agoriad (a) key *(more common in North Wales)*
allwedd (a) key *(more common in South Wales)*
amlen (an) envelope
anrheg (a) gift, present

b
babi (a) baby
bachgen (a) boy
bag (a) bag
balŵn (a) balloon
banana (a) banana
bara bread
bàth (a) bath
beic (a) bike

blodyn (a) flower 🌼
brenin (a) king 👑
buwch (a) cow 🐄
bys (a) finger, toe ☝

c
cacen (a) cake 🎂
camera (a) camera 📷
cannwyll (a) candle 🕯
caws cheese 🧀
ceffyl (a) horse 🐎
ceg (a) mouth 👄
ci (a) dog 🐶
clo (a) lock 🔒
cloc (a) clock 🕐
clust (a) ear 👂
coeden (a) tree 🌳
crys (a) shirt 👕
cwmwl (a) cloud ☁
cwpan (a) cup ☕
cyfrifiadur (a) computer 💻
cyllell (a) knife 🔪

ch
chwaer (a) sister
chwaraewr (a) player
chwarel (a) quarry
chwiban (a) whistle

d
dafad (a) sheep 🐑
darlun (an) illustration

desg (a) desk
diod (a) drink
diwrnod (a) day
drws (a) door 🚪
dyn (a) man 👨

e
e-bost (an) email
eglwys (a) church
eira snow
enfys (a) rainbow 🌈
esgid (a) shoe 👞

f
fan (a) van
feiolin (a) violin
ficer (a) vicar

ff
ffair (a) fair
ffenestr (a) window
ffôn (a) phone ☎
fforc (a) fork
ffrog (a) frock 👗

g
gafr (a) goat
gardd (a) garden
glaw rain
gwaed blood
gwely (a) bed 🛏
gwên (a) smile 🙂

23

gwlân wool
gwobr (a) prize 🏆

h
hanner half ½
haul (a) sun ☼
het (a) hat 👒
hosan (a) sock

i
iâ ice
iâr (a) hen 🐔
injan (an) engine

j
jam jam (traffic; preserve)
jar (a) jar
jeli (a) jelly
jwg (a) jug

l
lamp (a) lamp
lolipop (a) lollipop
lorri (a) lorry

ll
llaw (a) hand ✋
lleuad (a) moon 🌙
llun (a) photograph,
picture 🖼
llwy (a) spoon 🥄
llyfr (a) book 📖

llygad (an) eye 👁
llygoden (a) mouse 🐭
llythyr (a) letter 📩

m
mab (a) son 👦
mam (a) mother 👩
mam-gu (a) grandmother
👵 *(South Wales form)*
menyw (a) woman 👩
merch (a) girl, daughter 👧
mochyn (a) pig 🐷
modrwy (a) ring 💍
morthwyl (a) hammer 🔨

n
nain (a) grandmother 👵
(North Wales form)
neidr (a) snake
nionyn (an) onion *(North Wales form)*
nyth (a) nest

o
oen (a) lamb
ofn fear, fright 🙀
olwyn (a) wheel
oren (an) orange

p
pabell (a) tent
papur (a) paper

24

parsel (a) parcel
pêl (a) ball
pensil (a) pencil
piano (a) piano
pysgodyn (a) fish

r
radio (a) radio
roced (a) rocket
rygbi rugby

rh
rhaff (a) rope
rhaw (a) shovel
rheilffordd (a) railway
rhosyn (a) rose
rhyngrwyd Internet

s
sbectol glasses, spectacles
sebon soap
seren (a) star
sgert (a) skirt
sgwâr (a) square
siop (a) shop
siswrn scissors
sosban (a) saucepan

t
tad (a) father
tad-cu (a) grandfather
(South Wales form)

tafod (a) tongue
taid (a) grandfather *(North Wales form)*
tân (a) fire
taten (a) potato
teisen (a) cake
teledu (a) television
teulu (a) family
toiled (a) toilet
ton (a) wave
trwyn (a) nose

th
theatr (a) theatre
thermomedr (a) thermometer

u
uwd porridge

w
wal (a) wall
watsh (a) watch
wy (an) egg
wyneb (a) face

y
ynys (an) island
ysbyty (a) hospital
ysgol (a) school
ystafell (a) room

Exercise

1. Work your way through the coloured Emojis learning the word.
2. Go to the black and white Emojis and say/write the Welsh word **and** its colour – '*noun name*' and **glas** for gwrywaidd '*noun name*' and <u>**binc**</u> (mutated) for benywaidd.

Welsh word?

aderyn **glas**   — —————————

——————————   ——————————

allwedd **binc**   ——————————

——————————   ——————————

——————————   ——————————

——————————   ——————————

——————————   ——————————

——————————   ——————————

——————————   ——————————

——————————   ——————————

——————————   ——————————

——————————   ——————————

27

⚽ ———————————————

✏️ ———————————————

🐡 ———————————————

🕶️ ———————————————

💥 ———————————————

🛏️ ———————————————

✂️ ———————————————

👴 ———————————————

🔥 ———————————————

🍪 ———————————————

🎂 ———————————————

📺 ———————————————

👫 ———————————————

🚽 ———————————————

⌚ ———————————————

Welsh Word Gender (Gwrywaidd/Benywaidd)?

🦅	_____	✋	_____
🍎	_____	🧭	_____
🔑	_____	📷	_____
✉️	_____	🕯️	_____
🎁	_____	🧀	_____
👶	_____	🐴	_____
👦	_____	👄	_____
🏭	_____	🐕	_____
👂	_____	🔒	_____
🍌	_____	🕐	_____
🍞	_____	👂	_____
🛁	_____	🌳	_____
🚴	_____	👕	_____
🌼	_____	☕	_____
👑	_____	💻	_____
🐘	_____	🔪	_____

🔥 ———————————————   👪 ———————————————

🥔 ———————————————   🚽 ———————————————

🎂 ———————————————   ⌚ ———————————————

📺 ———————————————

Part 2

Describe and Do

This starts where Part 1 finished, with the basic sentence:

Mae'r + **f**erch + **f**ach a'r + bachgen + drwg a'r + ci + du a'r + **g**ath + **f**rown + **yn** + (**berfenw**) **cerdded** *(to walk)*.

In order to proceed you will need to learn:

* the contemporary, formal **Present Tense** of **bod** (*to be*); and
* the contemporary, formal **Imperfect Tense** of **bod**

By a process of simple substitution, you will then be able to construct:

Questions and **Negative** sentences for all Persons in **three** Tenses

because, by another simple substitution, you will also be able to create the **Perfect Tense** of **bod**.

Step 1
Learn the Present Tense of **bod**.

Present Tense Bod (*to be*)

rwyf fi/rydw i *I am*
rwyt ti *you are*
mae ef *he is*
mae hi *she is*

rydym ni/rydyn ni *we are*
rydych chi *you are*
maen nhw *they are*

These forms of **bod** will be the basis for what follows.
In the basic sentence: **Mae'r ferch fach yn cerdded**, you will see
that 'mae' is the 3rd person singular of the Present Tense of **'bod'**.

You now simply replace the **'mae'** form with another Person:
Mae'r ferch fach yn cerdded becomes
Mae hi'n cerdded. *She walks/She is walking*

Rwyf fi'n cerdded.
Rydym ni'n cerdded.

\|/

In the same way as **yr** contracts to **'r** after a vowel,
so **yn** following a vowel contracts to **'n**

fi/i + yn	**fi'n/i'n**
ti + yn	**ti'n**
ef/e + yn	**e'n**
hi + yn	**hi'n**
ni + yn	**ni'n**
chi + yn	**chi'n**
nhw + yn	**nhw'n**
teulu + yn	**teulu'n**

In a further contraction, the most heavily used
Rwyf fi'n becomes **Rwy'n**.

Now learn the Imperfect Tense of **bod**.

Imperfect Tense Bod (*to be*)

roeddwn i *I was*	**roeddem ni** *we were*
roeddet ti *you were*	**roeddech chi** *you were*
roedd ef *he was*	**roedden nhw** *they were*
roedd hi *she was*	

Step 2

Questions

As you will see, to ask a question in the Present Tense all you have to do is omit '**r**' at the beginning of the verbs that you learned in Step 1.

The only new forms to learn are 'ydy' and 'ydyn'.

To ask a question in the Imperfect Tense simply omit the '**r**' at the beginning of the verbs that you learned in Step 1. Unlike the Present Tense there are no new forms to learn.

Present Tense

wyf fi/ydw i *am I?*
wyt ti *are you?*
ydy ef *is he?*
ydy hi *Is she?*

ydym ni/ydyn ni *are we?*
ydych chi *are you?*
ydyn nhw *are they?*

Ydych chi a'r ferch fach yn mynd?
Ydy'r ferch fach yn dod?

Imperfect Tense

oeddwn i *was I?*
oeddet ti *were you?*
oedd ef *was he?*
oedd hi *was she?*

oeddem ni *were we?*
oeddech chi *were you?*
oedden nhw *were they?*

Oedd y ferch fach a'r bachgen yn mynd?

Not

To **form a negative verb,** replace the **'r'** at the beginning of 'rwyf', 'roeddwn', etc. with '**Nid**' or '**D - - - ddim**'

Present Tense

Using **wyf/yw**

nid wyf fi *I'm not*
nid wyt ti *you're not*
nid yw ef *he's not*
nid yw hi *she's not*

nid ydym ni *we're not*
nid ydych chi *you're not*
nid ydyn nhw *they aren't*

Using **ydw/ydy** add '**ddim**'

dwyf fi ddim/dydw i ddim
dwyt ti ddim
dyw e/dydy e ddim
dyw hi/dydi hi ddim

dydyn ni ddim
dydych chi ddim
dydyn nhw ddim

Nid yw'r ferch fach yn mynd. Dyw/Dydy'r ferch fach ddim yn mynd.
Nid ydych chi a'r ferch fach yn mynd. Dydych chi a'r ferch fach ddim yn mynd.

There are no exceptions in the **Imperfect Tense**

nid oeddwn i *I wasn't*
nid oeddet ti *you weren't*
nid oedd ef *he wasn't*
nid oedd hi *she wasn't*

doeddwn i ddim
doeddet ti ddim
doedd e ddim
doedd hi ddim

nid oeddem ni *we weren't*   **doedden ni ddim**
nid oeddech chi *you weren't*   **doeddech chi ddim**
nid oedden nhw *they weren't* **doedden nhw ddim**

Nid oedd y ferch fach yn mynd. Doedd y ferch fach ddim yn mynd.
Nid oeddwn i a'r ferch fach yn mynd. Doeddwn i a'r ferch fach ddim yn mynd.

A further simple substitution will add another tense to your armoury:

To create the **Perfect Tense** (*I have* 'seen', *you have* 'seen', *he/she has* 'seen', etc.)
Replace **yn** in the **Present Tense** of '**bod**' (*Rwyf fi **yn** gweld,* etc.) with **wedi**: *Rwyf fi **wedi** gweld (y ffilm).*

This is the **Perfect Tense**:

*Rwyf fi **wedi**...* (I have)
  Wyf fi wedi...? **Nid** *wyf fi wedi.../Dwyf fi ddim wedi.../Dydw i ddim wedi...*
*Rwyt ti **wedi*** (you have)
*Mae ef/hi **wedi**...* (he/she has)
  Ydy *ef/hi wedi...?* **Nid yw** *ef/hi wedi.../Dyw e/hi ddim wedi...*
*Rydym ni **wedi**...* (we have)
*Rydych chi **wedi**...* (you have)
*Maen nhw **wedi**...* (they have)
  Ydyn *nhw wedi...?* **Nid ydyn** *nhw wedi.../Dydyn nhw ddim wedi...*

You are now in a position to be able to use the list of feminine and masculine **enwau** together with the extended list of **ansoddeiriau** and **berfenwau** (p. 39) to create sentences using

36

all Persons of the *Present, Imperfect* and *Perfect* Tenses. Here are a few examples:

Roedd John a Jane yn mynd.
Rwyf fi a'r ci'n cerdded.
Nid oedden nhw'n canu/ Doedden nhw ddim yn canu
Wyt ti a'r teulu'n dod?
Nid yw ef wedi mynd/ Dyw e ddim wedi mynd
Ydyn nhw wedi mynd?

These sentences require one other ingredient: a sprinkling of **prepositions** – little words like *to, from, under, over* – that <u>follow</u> the verb-noun and <u>precede</u> a noun and show the relationship between the verb-noun **(berfenw)** and the noun **(enw)**.

Take three prepositions that trigger **Treiglad Meddal**:
i *to*
o *from*
dros *over*

Roedd John a Jane yn mynd **i** *Gaerdydd.*
Rwyf fi a'r ci yn cerdded **dros** *y bont.*
Wyt ti a'r teulu yn dod **i**'*r ffair?*
Nid yw ef wedi mynd **o**'*r tŷ/ Dyw e ddim wedi mynd* **o**'*r tŷ. Dydy e ddim wedi mynd* **o**'*r tŷ*
Ydyn nhw wedi mynd **i**'*r siop?*

The Prepositions

The following common prepositions in Welsh trigger **Treiglad Meddal** in the nouns that follow them:

am = *at*	**dros** = *over*	**heb** = *without*	**hyd** = *until*
ar = *on*	**drwy** = *through*	**i** = *to*	**wrth** = *from*
at = *(up) to*	**dan** = *under*	**o** = *from*	**gan** = *with*

37

They are printed in pink here because they trigger a mutation but **they are not nouns**, and elsewhere in this manual they will be printed in black.

Earlier you learned the useful little rhyme to help you with Treiglad Meddal:

C	P	T
G	B	D
Ll	M	Rh

Learning the following jingle will also pay dividends in the future:

Am, ar, at,
dros, drwy, dan
heb, i, o
hyd, wrth, gan

The way to do it is:

1. Type or write
   Am, ar, at,
   dros, drwy, dan
   heb, i, o
   hyd, wrth, gan
   recite it!

2. Hide **Am,**
   –, ar, at,
   dros, drwy, dan
   heb, i, o
   hyd, wrth, gan
   recite it in full.

Keep hiding one preposition at a time and recite the whole rhyme each time you do so.

Describe and Do

A basic list of (mutatable) adjectives (**ansoddeiriau**) and verb-nouns (**berfenwau**)

\|/
You will see that the single letters of the alphabet follow the same order as the English alphabet. However, the Welsh 'double' letters are in fact separate letters in their own right which follow the initial single letter (except in the case of 'ng').

achub follows **actio**
addo follows **adio**
anghofio follows **agor** and precedes **anfon**

a
actio to act
achub to save
adeiladu to build
adio to add
addo to promise
agor to open
anghofio to forget
anfon to send
aros to wait
arwain to lead

b
bach small
baglu to trip

bendigedig fantastic
berwi to boil
blasus tasty
blêr untidy
blino to tire
boddi to drown
bownsio to bounce
brown brown
brwnt dirty (S. Wales)
brwsio to brush
brysio to hurry
budr dirty (N. Wales)
bwrw[1] to hit
bwrw[2] to rain
bwyta to eat

39

byr short
byw to live

c
cadw to keep
caled hard
canu to sing
caredig kind
cario to carry
caru to love
cas nasty
cau to shut
cerdded to walk
cicio to kick
clapio to clap
cloi to lock
clymu to tie
coch red
codi to lift
cofio to remember
crafu to scratch
credu to believe
crio to cry
cryf strong
cuddio to hide
cwympo to fall
cyflym quick
cymysgu to mix
cynnar early
cynnes warm
cysgu to sleep
cytuno to agree

ch
chwarae to play
chwerthin to laugh
chwythu to blow

d
da good
dal to catch
darllen to read
dawnsio to dance
dechrau to start
digwydd to happen
dihuno to wake
diog lazy
diogel safe
disglair bright
distaw quiet
dod to come
dringo to climb
drwg bad
du black
dweud to say
dwfn deep

e
edrych to look
eistedd to sit
ennill to win

ff
ffonio to phone
ffrwydro to explode

g
galw to call
garw rough
glân clean
glanhau to clean
glas blue
gofalu to take care
gofyn to ask
golau light (of colour)
golchi to wash
gorffen to finish
gorwedd to lie down
gwag empty
gwan weak
gwasgu to squeeze
gweddïo to pray
gweiddi to shout
gwerthu to sell
gwisgo to dress
gwlyb wet
gwneud to do
gwrando to listen
gwybod to know
gwyllt wild

h
hedfan to fly
helpu to help
hoffi to like
holi to enquire

ll
llawn full
llefain to cry

llenwi to fill
lliwio to colour
llosgi to burn
llwyd grey
llydan wide
llyfn smooth

m
marw to die
mawr big
meddwl to think
melyn yellow
melys sweet
methu to fail
mynd to go

n
neidio to jump
newid to change
nofio to swim

p
paratoi to prepare
parcio to park
peintio to paint
pert pretty
pinc pink
plygu to bend
poeni to worry
poeth hot
posibl possible
priodi to marry

rh
rhad cheap
rhannu to divide
rhedeg to run
rhoi to give
rhwydd easy
rhyfedd strange

s
saethu to shoot
sefyll to stand
siarad to speak
siglo to shake
sychu to dry
symud to move

t
taflu to throw
taro to hit

tawel quiet
teimlo to feel
tenau thin
tew fat
tlawd poor
torri to break
trefnu to arrange
trist sad
tyfu to grow
tynnu to pull

y
yfed to drink
ymarfer to practise
ymladd to fight
ysgrifennu to write

Part 3

In the Workshop

The next stage of development will build on the foundations laid down in Parts 1 and 2 and show you how the **Past Tense** works. This tense is important in creating a narrative (telling the tale) in Welsh.

The differences between Welsh and English and indeed other European languages will now become more pronounced and, just as you have become accustomed to **Treiglad Meddal**, you will need to be patient and come to terms with other differences.

> \|/
> At this stage you need to get used to the term **berfenw** as in Welsh it is not the same as a '**verb**'. In the following section both the **berfenw** and its corresponding **verb** forms are printed in green.

Step 1 This labels the components you need and gives you tips on how to use them.

Step 2 This introduces the **Past Tense**, exemplifying the 'short' or 'conjugated' form of the verb.

Step 3 This deals with the **Subject** and **Object** of a sentence and how they are treated in Welsh.

These steps are followed by **Nuts, Bolts, Cogs and Springs** where you will find:

1. A basic list of the **little words** that help to hold sentences together
2. Lists of Welsh **Mutations**
3. **Personal pronouns**

Step 1

Here are the technical terms for the components you are now using.

1. The name of an action, or the **infinitive** form of the verb, is introduced in English by 'to' – *to run, to sing, to be*. In Welsh we translate 'infinitive' as **berfenw**. **Berfenwau** fulfil the same function as infinitives in English, but with one major difference – the 'to' element in English is built into the **berfenw**:

rhedeg = *to run*
canu = *to sing*
bod = *to be*

\|/
When translating *to run, to sing, to be*, etc. do <u>not</u> use 'i redeg', 'i ganu', 'i fod','etc.

2. **Berf** (y **f**erf) is translated as 'verb' in English. It is a form of the **berfenw** that tells us:
when an action takes place (Past, Present, etc.)
who undertakes the action (*fi, ti, hi, nhw*, etc.)

There are **two** ways to indicate the 'who' and 'when' in Welsh.

You have already learned how to use the long form, e.g. *Rwyf fi'n canu.*

who? 1st **Person** 'I' (fi)
when? the **Present** Tense of *bod* (rwyf)
'I am singing'.

\|/
The technical word for the long form of the verb is 'periphrastic', and the short form may be called 'inflected' or 'conjugated'.

Step 2

Another way of doing this is to use the 'short' forms of the **berf**.

To conjugate a **berf**:

1. Remove the ending of the **berfenw** (while noting that there are a few **berfenwau** with no such detachable ending, e.g. *edrych*)

2. Add a verb ending to the remaining stem (or directly to the end of the berfenw where there is no detachable ending) to indicate the Person undertaking the action.

Each tense has its own set of endings.
The endings for the **Past Tense** are:

1st Person singular	- **ais (i)**
2nd Person singular	- **aist (ti)**
3rd Person singular	- **odd (ef/hi)**
1st Person plural	- (a)**som (ni)**
2nd Person plural	- (a)**soch (chi)**
3rd Person plural	- (a)**sant (hwy/nhw)**

\|/
Please remember (and this is important) that the pronouns *i, ti, ef, hi,* etc. are placed in brackets **because the personal form is built into the verb ending** 'cofiais' = **I** remembered.

3. So!

Take:
cofio to remember   **credu** to believe

i. Remove the ending from the **berfenw**, leaving the stem of the **berf**:

cofi •   **cred** •

Add the endings for the Past Tense:

Singular	Plural
1st Person	
cofi**ais** *I remembered*	cofia**som** *we remembered*
2nd Person	
cofi**aist** *you remembered*	cofia**soch** *you remembered*
3rd Person	
cofi**odd** *he/she remembered*	cofia**sant** *they remembered*
cred**ais** *believed*	creda**som** *we believed*
cred**aist** *you believed*	creda**soch** *you believed*
cred**odd** *he/she believed*	creda**sant** *they believed*

There are equivalent (but different) endings for all the verb Tenses in Welsh, which are added in the same way as these endings in the Past Tense.

The Past Tense

Take the following berfenwau:

		stem
adeiladu	*to build*	adeilad •
cerdded	*to walk*	cerdd •
addurno	*to decorate*	addurn •
gwisgo	*to wear*	gwisg •
cwympo	*to fall*	cwymp •
edrych	*to look*	drych •

\I/
There are complications involved in the use of the plural forms. Here we shall concentrate on the more regular singular forms.

and translate the following verbs into Welsh:

I built
he/she walked
you decorated
he/she wore
I fell
he/she fell
you looked

Then have a go at translating the following sentences:

The little girl walked over the bridge.
I decorated the tree.
She wore a red hat.
He fell over the stone.

Step 3

berf: Subject and Object

We've looked at the **'when'** of 'y ferf'. This is the **'Tense'** involved (Past, Present, etc.).

We've looked at the **'who'** of 'y ferf'. This is the **'Person'** involved (1st Person 'I', 2nd Person 'You', etc.), the one who <u>does</u> the action.

But there is another **'who'** or **'what'** involved – the one <u>affected</u> by the action.

The **'who'** who **does** the action is known as the **subject** of the berf ('goddrych' in Welsh).

The **'who'** or **'what' affected by** the action is known as the **object** of the berf ('gwrthrych' in Welsh).

What follows is applied instinctively by a native Welsh speaker in the same way as the other mutations that you have learned.

In English, the difference between the role of subject and object in a sentence doesn't lead to the change that occurs in Welsh. This is why we will concentrate in some detail on how to distinguish between the **subject** of a verb and its **object**.

The key!

To determine the **subject** of a sentence, ask **who/what** directly **before** the berf.
To determine the **object** of a sentence, ask **who/what** directly **after** the berf.

'John kicked the ball.'

who kicked?   John (the **subject**)
kicked **what**?   the ball (the **object**)

In Welsh, the order of the sentence may be different, but the same technique applies.

'Ciciodd John y bêl.'

ciciodd (3rd Person Singular, Past Tense of **cicio**)
who ciciodd?   John (the **subject**)
ciciodd **what**?   y bêl (the **object**)

It can't be that simple – can it?

Well, yes and no. This is where those hidden parts come into play.

\|/
'**a**': a noun on its own in Welsh includes 'a/an': **cath** = **a** cat
'**I, you, he**' etc.: the ending of the short form **berf** (of the verb) includes the Person: **Cerddais** = **I** walked

---

48

Here comes the significance of all this.

> When the short form of any **berf** and its **subject** (whether expressed or not, i.e. *'ciciodd'*, or *'ciciodd John'*) is followed directly by the **object** 'pêl' (**not** y̱ bêl) it triggers our old friend **Treiglad Meddal**.

In order to translate: **He kicked a̱ ball**

1. **who** ciciodd? ciciodd (*ef*) (the **subject** in this instance is built into the 'berf')
2. ciciodd **what?** pêl (the **object**) (**a** *ball*)

This gives

CICIODD BÊL: CICIODD EF BÊL: CICIODD JOHN BÊL

Subject and **Object** refer to the job or function of a word in a sentence, not to its meaning. So the same word may be a subject in one sentence and an object in another.

Can you see this in:

gwelodd ci gath: and **gwelodd cath gi.**

This may seem confusing at first, but it's worth getting to grips with the difference.

(**who** *gwelodd*? *gwelodd* **what**?)

Gwelais y bachgen (pink and blue rules)
Gwelais fachgen (Subject Object rules)
Gwelais y ferch (pink and blue rules)
Gwelais ferch (Subject Object rules)

I sang a song canais gân
The dog saw a cat gwelodd y ci gath
The team praised a supporter canmolodd y tîm gefnogwr

Read the following:

Gwel**odd** Dafydd (*subject*) **dd**yn (*object*) yn cerdded dros y bont. Dilyn**odd** Dafydd (*subject*) y dyn a gwelodd y dyn yn edrych ar (*preposition*) **g**ar coch newydd. Tynn**odd** y dyn (*subject*) **f**orthwyl (*object*) o (*preposition*) **f**ag. Torr**odd** ffenestr y car.

Continue this exciting tale – or start your own novel.

Step 4

Nuts, Bolts, Cogs and Springs

This is a list of those little words that hold sentences together. One of the problems is that the same little word can be used in more than one way, and it can trigger a different mutation depending on how it is used.

> \|/
> Be patient, take a group at a time until you are happy you understand the differences. 'How do you eat an elephant?' One chunk at a time.

a
There are three types of **a** in Welsh.

a¹ The first 'a' means *and*. You used this in Part 1 in phrases such as 'y bachgen bach **a**'r ferch fawr'. You need to be aware of two other features of this '**a**'.

- **a** becomes **ac** before a vowel *afal* **ac** *oren*
- **a** triggers another mutation, **Treiglad Llaes** (the Spirant Mutation).

Fortunately, this only affects three letters:

C becomes **Ch**
P becomes **Ph**
T becomes **Th**

a dog and *a cat* = ci **a** chath
a river and *a bridge* = afon **a** phont
a shop and *a house* = siop **a** thŷ

- Look up any noun (as above), berfenw or adjective beginning with C, P, T and link them to another word in the same category with this **a:** adrodd **a** chanu; llawen **a** thrist

a² is the interrogative **A?** which is used to introduce a question.

When placed before the **short forms** of the verb, this '**A**' triggers **Treiglad Meddal**.

In this book we have only looked at short forms of the **Past Tense**.

Gwelodd John y ferch.   **A welodd** ef y ferch?
                                  A welaist ti y ferch?
                                  A welais i y ferch?

In formal, literary Welsh the '**A**' is often retained at the start of a question, but contemporary practice, both written and spoken, tends to omit it <u>but to keep the mutation</u> *'Welaist ti'r ferch?'*

a³ is the relative pronoun 'that' or 'who'. This **'a'** also triggers **Treiglad Meddal**.

y ci **a w**elodd y gath (*the dog* **that** *saw the cat*)
y dyn **a g**usanodd y ferch (*the man* **who** *kissed the girl*)

In summary:

a conjunction *and* becomes

ac before a vowel   triggers **Treiglad Llaes**

a interrogative particle   triggers **Treiglad Meddal**

a relative pronoun   triggers **Treiglad Meddal**

Yn
There are three types of **'yn'** in Welsh.

yn¹ This is the 'yn' used before the **berfenw** as in *Rwyf fi* **yn** *mynd*.

- It contracts to **'n** in *Rwyt ti'n, Mae hi'n (mynd)*, etc.
- It does **not** trigger a mutation.

yn² is the preposition **yn** 'in'. It is frequently used before place-names.

Mae ef yn byw **yn** *Ynys-y-bŵl. Mae castell* **yn** *Harlech a phrifysgol* **yn** *Aberystwyth.*

- This 'yn' does **not** contract to **'n**.
- It triggers **Treiglad Trwynol**. (See p. 57 for this mutation and some examples of its use.)

yn³ is the predicative 'yn'.

- This is the adverbial 'yn' used to introduce *'is'* before an

adjective following a verb: *Mae Siân* **yn** *dda* (Siân is good) *Mae'r ci* **yn** *ddrwg* (The dog is bad)
- This 'yn' triggers **Treiglad Meddal** with the exception of 'll' and 'rh'
- It contracts to **'n** in *Mae hi'n* **dda**, *Mae e'n* **ddrwg**.
- It is also used to introduce *'is a'* before a noun *Mae Siân* **yn** *wraig.* (Siân is a wife.) *Mae'r ci* **yn** *gorgi.* (The dog is a corgi.)
- It contracts to **'n** in *Mae'n wraig. Mae'n gorgi. Mae'n ddau o'r gloch.*

In summary:

Mae Mair **yn** + *darllen*

Mae Mair **yn** + *dda*

Mae Mair **yn** + *ferch*

Mae Mair **yn(g)** = *Nghaerdydd*

Personal Pronouns

1. You already know the **affixed** personal pronouns

fi/i	*I*
ti/di	*you*
ef/e	*he*
hi	*she*
ni	*we*
chi	*you*
nhw	*they*

so called because they always <u>follow</u> the verb to denote the **subject**, as in *rwyf* **fi**, *rydych* **chi**, etc.

The **independent** personal pronouns are very similar:

mi, fi	*me*	**ni**	*us*
ti, di	*you*	**chi**	*you*
ef/fe/fo	*him*	**nhw**	*them*
hi	*her*		

- these are used to denote the **object** *gwelais i **ef/chi/nhw*** etc.
- they are so called because they can <u>stand alone</u> and represent both **subject** and **object**

2. You now need the **prefixed (or possessive) pronouns**: so called because the are used <u>before</u> the verb and nouns:

fy	*my*	**ein**	*our*
dy	*your*	**eich**	*your*
ei	*his*	**eu**	*their*
ei	*her*		

In order to use these you will need to make use of all the mutations (see p. 57):

---

fy (*my*) triggers **Treiglad Trwynol**
dy (*your*) triggers **Treiglad Meddal**
ei *(his)* triggers **Treiglad Meddal**
ei *(her)* triggers **Treiglad Llaes** and **H** before a vowel

ein *(our)* triggers **H** before a vowel
eich *(your)* **NO MUTATION**
eu *(their)* triggers **H** before a vowel

Treiglad Trwynol (Nasal Mutation)

Treiglad Trwynol occurs following **fy** (= my) and **yn** (= in). It affects words beginning with the letters C, P, T, G, B and D.

c	→	**ngh**
p	→	**mh**
t	→	**nh**
g	→	**ng**
b	→	**m**
d	→	**n**

1. fy

cath (cat)　　　　　fy **ngh**ath
• translate *my chair; my camera; my cap*

pont (bridge)　　　fy **mh**ont
• translate *my ball; my pencil; my piano*

tref (town)　　　　fy **nh**ref (town)
• translate *my father; my television; my family*

gardd (garden)　　fy **ng**ardd
• translate *my garage; my game; my hair*

bachgen (boy)　　fy **m**achgen
• translate *my bag; my balloon; my bat*

drws (door)　　　fy **n**rws
• translate *my sheep; my desk; my drink*

You will hear that this mutation can turn English-sounding words like 'garej' into something quite different like 'ngarej'.

2. yn (= 'in')

Things become a little more complicated when you use **Treiglad Trwynol** after 'yn', since 'yn' can also change its form when followed by this mutation. Fortunately, it's not all doom and gloom as:

yn remains unchanged before **T** and **D**
yn Nhorfaen
yn Nyffryn Nantlle

However, it becomes:

yng before **C** and **G**
yng Nghaernarfon
yng Ngwauncaegurwen

and:

ym before **P** and **B**
ym Mhontypridd
ym Mangor

Complete:

yn + Casnewydd (Newport)
yn + Cricieth

yn + Glynllifon
yn + Glynebwy (Ebbw Vale)

yn + Beddgelert
yn + Boncath

yn + Pontyberem
yn + Prestatyn

\|/
Remember this 'yn' means 'in' in English. There are two other types of 'yn' and these are explained on page 52. They do not trigger **Treiglad Trwynol**.

The Aspirate 'H'

This just means that you have to add an 'h' before vowels following these three personal pronouns:

ei (feminine)   *her*
ein   *our*
eu   *their*

ei **h**athro (*her teacher*)
ein **h**eglwys (*our church*)

\|/
Remember that as well as **a, e, i, o, u** the letters **w** and **y** are also vowels in Welsh.

eu **h**athro (*their teacher*)
eu **h**injan dân (*their fire-engine*)
ei **h**oren (*her orange*)
ein **h**uwd (*our porridge*)
ein **h**ysgol (*our school*)
ei **h**wyres (*her granddaughter*)

You will also come across this 'h' when you learn certain numerals, e.g. *un ar hugain, dau ar hugain,* etc. Go to page 58 if you want to know more.

Mutations summary

Treiglad Meddal			Treiglad Trwynol		Treiglad Llaes	
C	**G**	y gath	**Ngh**	fy nghath	**Ch**	ei chath
P	**B**	gwelais bont	**Mh**	ym Mhontypridd	**Ph**	ei phont
T	**D**	y delyn fach	**Nh**	fy nhelyn fach	**Th**	feiolin a thelyn
G	–	dy ardd	**Ng**	fy ngardd		
B	**F**	ei frawd	**M**	ym Mlaenau Ffestiniog		
D	**Dd**	dy ddafad	**N**	fy nafad		
Ll	**L**	ei long				
M	**F**	carodd ferch				
Rh	**R**	dy ruban				

Aspirate Mutation (H before vowels)

a	ei **h**athro
e	ein **h**eglwys
i	eu **h**injan dân
o	ei **h**oren
u	ein **h**uwd
w*	ein **h**wyres
y	ein **h**ysgol

> \I/
> There is a 'w' in Welsh which acts as a vowel as in *wyres*; and a 'w' which acts as a consonant as in *watsh* – the latter does not trigger the 'h' (*ei watsh* = her watch).

Step 5
Back to verbs

> **Caveat!**
> *I appreciate this may be a step too far at this stage. I include it because I have failed to find an adequate explanation in any of the books of Welsh grammar with which I am acquainted.*

We now need to bring together all the things you have learned up to this point in order to negotiate one of the most tricky aspects of the **berf**.

The short/**conjugated** form of the **berf** makes use of the same Personal Pronouns – **fi, ti, ef, hi, ni, chi, nhw** – to refer to the **object** as well as the subject.

Well that's easy!

Gwelodd hi John/ gwelodd hi **ef** (*She saw John/him*)
Gwelais Mair/ gwelais **hi** (*I saw Mair/her*)
Clywsant gath/ clywsant **hi** (*They heard a cat/her/it*)

The obvious thing to do is to use the same construction with the long/periphrastic form of the verb and so form sentences such as:

Mae hi'n gweld y ci
Mae hi'n gweld **ef.**

But this is incorrect!!!

When using the long form of the verb to
translate sentences, such as *She sees him*,
you will have to use the prefixed or
possessive pronouns (page 54)
in conjunction with the **berfenw** to refer to the object.

Welsh has no single
form corresponding
to *me, you, him,
her, us, you, them,*
which are used in
English to refer to
the **object** of a
sentence.

	Subject	Object
Present Tense	**Long form**	
'*I see her*'	**Rwyf i̱ yn ei gweld (hi)**	
who? sees	(gweld) *i/fi:* sees (gweld) **whom?** *hi*	
'*We see you*'	Rydym **ni̱** yn **dy** weld (di)	
who? sees	(gweld) ***ni:*** sees (gweld) **whom?** *ti/di*	

Using:
1. the Present Tense of **Bod**
2. the possessive pronouns and the mutations they generate

construct

I see her
He hears me
He loves her
She loves him
They are watching (gwylio) *me*
We see them

Part 4

Numerals

Welsh has two number systems – traditional and modern. You need to learn the traditional system up to 30 in order to tell the time (see p. 67). This book will only look at cardinal numbers, so you will see the word for 'twenty' but not for 'twentieth'. Dates will have to wait until another day!

We'll start with the numbers 1–10, as they are the same in both the traditional and modern systems. The following tables list the masculine and feminine forms and show you how to use them with the correct mutations.
(TM Treiglad Meddal; TLl Treiglad Llaes)

The Masculine Numerals

	Masculine	Mutation triggered	Example	Notes
0	dim			
1	un	none	un ci	
2	dau	TM	dau **gi**	'dau' mutates after 'y': y **dd**au **gi**
3	tri	TLl	tri **chi**	
4	pedwar	none	pedwar ci	
5	pump	none	pum ci	'pump' becomes 'pum' when placed directly before a noun
6	chwech	TLl	chwe **chi**	'chwech' becomes 'chwe' when placed directly before a noun

60

7	saith	none	saith ci	
8	wyth	none	wyth ci	yr wyth
9	naw	none	naw ci	
10	deg	none	deg ci	

The Feminine Numerals

	Feminine	Mutation triggered	Example	Notes
0	dim			
1	un	TM	un **g**ath	
2	dwy	TM	dwy **g**ath	'dwy' mutates after 'y': y **dd**wy **g**ath
3	tair	none	tair cath	although 'tair' is feminine it does not mutate after 'y'
4	pedair	none	pedair cath	although 'pedair' is feminine it does not mutate after 'y'
5	pump	none	pum cath	'pump' becomes 'pum' when placed directly before a noun
6	chwech	TLI	chwe chath	'chwech' becomes 'chwe' when placed directly before a noun
7	saith	none	saith cath	
8	wyth	none	wyth cath	
9	naw	none	naw cath	
10	deg	none	deg cath	

In Summary

Treiglad Meddal: dau and dwy following 'y'
Treiglad Meddal: nouns following dau and dwy
Treiglad Llaes: nouns following tri, chwe, chwe
pump, chwech become 'pum' and 'chwe' when placed before nouns
No mutation of tair and pedair following 'y'

As indicated above, matters become more complicated from 11 on. A simpler modern system means that you don't have to master the whole of the traditional system. However, the traditional system is alive and kicking, especially when telling the time, using dates and when writing sums of money.

The Choice of Numerical Systems

	Traditional	*Modern*	*Most common Example*	*Also acceptable: Example*
11	un ar ddeg	un deg un	un deg un o fechgyn, un deg un o ferched	un deg un bachgen un deg un ferch
12	deuddeg	un deg dau/dwy	un deg dau o lyfrau, un deg dwy o bunnoedd	
13	tri/tair ar ddeg	un deg tri/ tair	un deg tri o gŵn, un deg tair o ddefaid	
14	pedwar/ pedair ar ddeg	un deg pedwar/ pedair	un deg pedwar o fyrddau, un deg pedair o gadeiriau	
15	pymtheg	un deg pump		
16	un ar bymtheg	un deg chwech		

17	dau/ dwy ar bymtheg	un deg saith		
18	deunaw	un deg wyth		
19	pedwar/ pedair ar bymtheg	un deg naw		
20	ugain	dau ddeg	dau ddeg o fechgyn, dau ddeg o ferched	
21	un ar **h**ugain **Note**: Aspirate mutation here and in following	dau ddeg un	dau ddeg un o fechgyn, dau ddeg un o ferched	
22	dau/ dwy ar hugain	dau ddeg dau/dwy	dau ddeg dau o lyfrau, dau ddeg dwy o bunnoedd	
23	tri/tair ar hugain	dau ddeg tri/tair	dau ddeg tri o gŵn, dau ddeg tair o ddefaid	
24	pedwar/ pedair ar hugain	dau ddeg pedwar/ pedair	dau ddeg pedwar o fyrddau, dau ddeg pedair o gadeiriau	
25	pump ar hugain	dau ddeg pump		
26	chwech ar hugain	dau ddeg chwech		
27	saith ar hugain	dau ddeg saith		
28	wyth ar hugain	dau ddeg wyth		
29	naw ar hugain	dau ddeg naw		
30	deg ar hugain	tri deg		

The traditional/formal numerical system 11–30

Masculine numerals

	Traditional	Mutation triggered	Example	Notes
11	un ar ddeg	none	un ci ar ddeg	'ar' triggers TM
12	deuddeg	none	deuddeg ci	
13	tri ar ddeg	TLI	tri **chi** ar ddeg	
14	pedwar ar ddeg	none	pedwar ci ar ddeg	
15	pymtheg	none	pymtheg ci	
16	un ar bymtheg		un ci ar bymtheg	
17	dau ar bymtheg	TM	dau **gi** ar bymtheg	'dau' mutates after 'y': y **dd**au **g**i ar bymtheg
18	deunaw	none	deunaw ci	
19	pedwar ar bymtheg	none	pedwar ci ar bymtheg	
20	ugain	none	ugain ci	
21	un ar hugain	none	un ci ar hugain	'ar' in this combination triggers an **Aspirate Mutation** (AM)
22	dau ar hugain	TM	dau **gi** ar hugain	TM after 'y'
23	tri ar hugain	TLI	tri **chi** ar hugain	
24	pedwar ar hugain	none	pedwar ci ar hugain	
25	pump ar hugain	none	pum ci ar hugain	'pump' becomes 'pum' when placed directly before a noun

26	chwech ar hugain	TLl	chwe **ch**i ar hugain	'chwech' becomes 'chwe' when placed directly before a noun
27	saith ar hugain	none	saith ci ar hugain	
28	wyth ar hugain	none	wyth ci ar hugain	yr wyth
29	naw ar hugain	none	naw ci ar hugain	
30	deg ar hugain	none	deg ci ar hugain	

Feminine **numerals**

	Traditional	*Mutation triggered*	*Example*	*Notes*
11	un ar ddeg	TM	un **g**ath ar ddeg	**'ar'** triggers TM
12	deuddeg	none	deuddeg cath	
13	tair ar ddeg	none	tair cath ar ddeg	although 'tair' is feminine it does <u>not</u> mutate after 'y': y tair cath
14	pedair ar ddeg	none	pedair cath ar ddeg	although 'pedair' is feminine it does <u>not</u> mutate after 'y': y pedair cath
15	pymtheg	none	pymtheg cath	
16	un ar bymtheg	TM	un **g**ath ar bymtheg	
17	dwy ar bymtheg	TM	dwy **g**ath ar bymtheg	**dwy** mutates after 'y'
18	deunaw	none	deunaw cath	

19	pedair ar bymtheg	none	pedair cath ar bymtheg	although 'pedair' is feminine it does not mutate after 'y': y pedair cath
20	ugain	none	ugain cath	
21	un ar hugain	TM	un **g**ath ar hugain	'ar' in this combination triggers an **Aspirate Mutation** (AM)
22	dwy ar hugain	TM	dwy **g**ath ar hugain	TM after 'y'
23	tair ar hugain	none	tair cath ar hugain	although 'tair' is feminine it does not mutate after 'y'
24	pedair ar hugain	none	pedair cath ar hugain	although 'pedair' is feminine it does not mutate after 'y'
25	pump ar hugain	none	pum cath ar hugain	'pump' becomes 'pum' when placed directly before a noun
26	chwech ar hugain	TLI	chwe **ch**ath ar hugain	'chwech' becomes 'chwe' when placed directly before a noun
27	saith ar hugain	none	saith cath ar hugain	
28	wyth ar hugain	none	wyth cath ar hugain	yr wyth
29	naw ar hugain	none	naw cath ar hugain	
30	deg ar hugain	none	deg cath ar hugain	

As a final flourish:

Before 'diwrnod' (day), 'blwydd' (year old) and 'blynedd' (year), a number of other forms are used:

deg → **deng** + TT	*deng: mlwydd: niwrnod: mlynedd*
deuddeg → **deuddeng** + TT	*deuddeng: mlwydd: niwrnod: mlynedd*
pymtheg → **pymtheng** + TT	*deuddeng: mlwydd: niwrnod: mlynedd*

Telling the Time

In order to **tell the time**, you need to know the masculine numerals from 1 to12 in the traditional/formal system.

1   **un** (o'r gloch)
2   **dau** (o'r gloch)
3   **tri** (o'r gloch)
4   **pedwar** (o'r gloch)
5   **pump** (o'r gloch)
6   **chwech** (o'r gloch)
7   **saith** (o'r gloch)
8   **wyth** (o'r gloch)
9   **naw** (o'r gloch)
10   **deg** (o'r gloch)
11   **un ar ddeg** (o'r gloch)
12   **deuddeg** (o'r gloch)

\|/
'at' one o'clock etc.
is introduced by **am**
which is followed by TM
am un o'r gloch
am ddau o'r gloch
am dri o'r gloch
am bedwar o'r gloch
am bump o'r gloch
am ddeg o'r gloch
am ddeuddeg o'r gloch

pink and **blue** nouns again

The gender of some nouns in Welsh is determined by where you live in Wales. The most prominent of these is 'munud' *minute* (of time) which is **masculine** in North Wales and **feminine** in the South.

North *masculine*	South *feminine*	*i (to)* *wedi (past)*
un munud	un **f**unud	*i/ wedi*
dau **f**unud	dwy **f**unud	*i/ wedi*
tri munud	tair munud	*i/ wedi*
pedwar munud	pedair munud	*i/ wedi*
pum munud	pum munud	*i/ wedi*
chwe munud	chwe munud	*i/ wedi*
saith munud	saith munud	*i/ wedi*
wyth munud	wyth munud	*i/ wedi*
naw munud	naw munud	*i/ wedi*
deng munud	deng munud	*i/ wedi*
un munud ar ddeg	un funud ar ddeg	*i/ wedi*
deuddeg munud	deuddeg munud	*i/ wedi*
tri munud ar ddeg	tair munud ar ddeg	*i/ wedi*
pedwar munud ar ddeg	pedair munud ar ddeg	*i/ wedi*
chwarter	chwarter	*i/ wedi*
un munud ar bymtheg	un **f**unud ar bymtheg	*i/ wedi*
dau **f**unud ar bymtheg	dwy **f**unud ar bymtheg	*i/ wedi*
deunaw munud	deunaw munud	*i/ wedi*
pedwar munud ar bymtheg	pedair munud ar bymtheg	*i/ wedi*
ugain munud	ugain munud	*i/ wedi*
un munud ar hugain	un **f**unud ar hugain	*i/ wedi*
dau **f**unud ar hugain	dwy **f**unud ar hugain	*i/ wedi*
tri munud ar hugain	tair munud ar hugain	*i/ wedi*
pedwar munud ar hugain	pedair munud ar hugain	*i/ wedi*
pum munud ar hugain	pum munud ar hugain	*i/ wedi*

chwe munud ar hugain	chwe munud ar hugain	*i/ wedi*
saith munud ar hugain	saith munud ar hugain	*i/ wedi*
wyth munud ar hugain	wyth munud ar hugain	*i/ wedi*
naw munud ar hugain	naw munud ar hugain	*i/ wedi*
hanner awr	hanner awr	*wedi*

yr oriau (the hours)
un, dau, tri, pedwar, pump, chwech, etc.

Mae'n dri o'r gloch

Mae'n ddau funud wedi tri N*orth*
Mae'n ddwy funud wedi tri *South*

Mae'n chwarter wedi tri **N** & **S**

Mae'n un munud ar hugain wedi tri **N**
Mae'n un funud ar hugain wedi tri **S**

Mae'n hanner awr wedi tri **N** & **S**

Mae'n dri munud ar hugain i bedwar **N**
Mae'n dair munud ar hugain i bedwar **S**

Mae'n chwarter i bedwar **N** & **S**

 Mae'n bedwar munud i bedwar **N**
Mae'n bedair munud i bedwar **S**

 Mae'n ddeng munud i bedwar **N** & **S**

 Mae'n ddeng munud wedi pedwar **N** & **S**

Part 5

Y Geiriadur (English–Welsh)

The following letters indicate the mutation triggered by the word:

TM   Treiglad Meddal
TLl Treiglad Llaes

TT   Treiglad Trwynol
H   H before a vowel

The colour code:
enw = noun masculine *bachgen*
enw = **noun feminine** *merch*
enw = **noun plural** *newyddion*
enw = **noun masculine** or **noun feminine**
(depending on North Wales or South Wales, e.g. **munud**; or on the gender, e.g. **nyrs** (male or female), though this is rare.)
ansoddair = adjective *bach*
berfenw = verb-noun *canu*

able (to be) **gallu**
about **am**; **ar** TM
above **uwchben**
accept (to) **derbyn**
act (to) **actio**
add (to) **adio**
admire (to) **edmygu**
adult **oedolyn** (oedolion)
aeroplane **awyren** (awyrennau)
after **wedi**
afternoon **prynhawn**
  (prynhawniau)
afterwards **wedyn**
again **eto**
age **oed:oedran**
agree (to) **cytuno**
ahead **ymlaen**

all **i gyd**
also **hefyd**
amazed (to be) **rhyfeddu**
ambulance **ambiwlans**
  (ambiwlansys)
anchor **angor** (angorau)
and **a¹** TLl
angel **angel** (angylion)
angry **dig**
angry (to become) **digio**
animal **anifail** (anifeiliaid)
answer **ateb** (atebion)
answer (to) **ateb**
any **unrhyw**
apologize (to) **ymddiheuro**
apple **afal** (afalau)
appoint (to) **penodi**

April **Ebrill, mis Ebrill**
arm **braich** (breichiau)
as **â²** TLl
as **cyn²** TM
ask (to) **gofyn**
astonishing **rhyfeddol**
at **am** TM; **ar** TM
August **Awst, mis Awst**
aunt **modryb** (modrybedd)
autumn **hydref** (hydrefau)
awful **ofnadwy**

baby **babi** (babis)
back **cefn** (cefnau)
backside **pen-ôl** (penolau)
bad **drwg**
bag **bag** (bagiau)
bake (to) **pobi**
ball **pêl** (peli)
balloon **balŵn** (balwnau)
banana **banana** (bananas)
basket **basged** (basgedi)
bat **bat** (batiau)
bath **bàth** (bathiau)
beach **traeth** (traethau)
because **oherwydd**
bed **gwely** (gwelyau:gwelâu)
beer **cwrw**
before **cyn¹**
begin (to) **dechrau**
believe (to) **credu**
bell **cloch** (clychau)
belly **bol:bola** (boliau)
belt **belt** (beltiau)

bend (to) **plygu**
best **gorau**
better **gwell**
between **rhwng**
big **mawr**
big toe **bawd**
bigger **mwy**
bike **beic** (beiciau)
bird **aderyn** (adar)
birth (to give) **geni**
birthday **pen blwydd:**
    pen-blwydd (pennau
    blwydd:penblwyddi)
bite (to) **cnoi**
black **du**
blacksmith **gof** (gofaint)
blame **bai** (beiau)
blanket **blanced** (blancedi)
blood **gwaed**
blow (to) **chwythu**
blue **glas**
board **bwrdd**
boat **cwch** (cychod)
bog **cors** (corsydd)
boil (to) **berwi**
bone **asgwrn** (esgyrn)
book **llyfr** (llyfrau)
boring **diflas**
bottle **potel** (poteli)
bottom **gwaelod** (gwaelodion)
box **bocs** (bocsys)
boy **bachgen** (bechgyn)
brain **ymennydd** (ymenyddiau:
    ymenyddion)

brave **dewr**
bread **bara**
break (to) **torri**
breakfast **brecwast** (brecwastau)
bridge **pont** (pontydd)
bright **disglair**
brown **brown**
brush (to) **brwsio**
build (to) **adeiladu**
burn (to) **llosgi**
busy **prysur**
but **ond**
butter **menyn**
buy (to) **prynu**
by **gan** TM

café **caffi** (caffis)
cake **cacen** (cacennau);
   teisen (teisennau)
call (to) **galw**
camera **camera** (camerâu)
candle **cannwyll** (canhwyllau)
cap **cap** (capiau)
capital (city) **prifddinas**
   (prifddinasoedd)
car **car** (ceir)
careful **gofalus**
carry (to) **cario**
castle **castell** (cestyll)
cat **cath** (cathod)
catch (to) **dal**
cattle **da**^{2}
cease **peidio**
celebrate (to) **dathlu**

ceremony **seremoni**
   (seremonïau)
chair **cadair** (cadeiriau)
change (to) **newid**
channel **sianel** (sianeli:
   sianelau)
chapel **capel** (capeli)
cheap **rhad**
cheek **boch** (bochau)
cheese **caws**
child **plentyn** (plant)
chocolate **siocled** (siocledi)
choir **côr** (corau)
choose (to) **dewis**
Christmas **Nadolig** (Nadoligau)
church **eglwys** (eglwysi)
cigarette **sigarét** (sigaretau)
circle **cylch** (cylchoedd)
city **dinas** (dinasoedd)
clap (to) **clapio**
class **dosbarth** (dosbarthiadau)
clean **glân**
climb (to) **dringo**
clock **cloc** (clociau)
clothes **dillad**
cloud **cwmwl** (cymylau)
coal **glo**
coat **cot:côt** (cotiau)
coffee **coffi**
cold **annwyd** (anwydau)
cold **oer**
colour **lliw** (lliwiau)
come (to) **dod**
comfortable **cyfforddus**

computer **cyfrifiadur**
(cyfrifiaduron)
cough **peswch**
cough (to) **pesychu**
country **gwlad** (gwledydd)
court **llys** (llysoedd)
cow **buwch** (buchod)
cream **hufen**
crowd **torf** (torfeydd)
cry (to) **crio; llefain**
cup **cwpan** (cwpanau)
cupboard **cwpwrdd** (cypyrddau)
cushion **clustog** (clustogau)
cycle (to) **seiclo**

daffodil **cenhinen Bedr**
daft **twp**
dance (to) **dawnsio**
dangerous **peryglus**
dark **tywyll**
daughter **merch** (merched)
day **diwrnod** (diwrnodau)
day **dydd** (dyddiau)
December **Rhagfyr,**
mis **Rhagfyr**
deep **dwfn**
desk **desg** (desgiau)
dessert **pwdin** (pwdinau)
dictionary **geiriadur**
(geiriaduron)
die (to) **marw**
different **gwahanol**
difficult **anodd**
dig (to) **palu**

dinner **cinio** (ciniawau)
dirt **baw**
dirty **brwnt; budr**
discover (to) **darganfod**
dishes **llestri**
divide (to) **rhannu**
do (to) **gwneud**
doctor **doctor** (doctoriaid);
meddyg (meddygon)
dog **ci** (cŵn)
door **drws** (drysau)
down **(i) lawr**
dragon **draig** (dreigiau)
draw (to) **tynnu**
dress (to) **gwisgo**
drink **diod** (diodydd)
drink (to) **yfed**
drive (to) **gyrru**
drown (to) **boddi**
dry **sych**
dry (to) **sychu**

ear **clust** (clustiau)
early **cynnar**
earth[1] **daear**[1]**; pridd**
(priddoedd)
Earth[2] **Daear**[2]
east **dwyrain**
easy **hawdd; rhwydd**
eat (to) **bwyta**
e-book **e-lyfr** (e-lyfrau)
egg **wy** (wyau)
eisteddfod **eisteddfod**
(eisteddfodau)

election **etholiad** (etholiadau)
electricity **trydan**
email **e-bost** (e-byst)
empty **gwag**
end **diwedd**
energy **egni**
engine **injan** (injans)
England **Lloegr**
English **Seisnig**
English (language) **Saesneg**
Englishman **Sais** (Saeson)
Englishwoman **Saesnes**
  (Saesnesau)
enjoy (to) **mwynhau**
enough **digon**
envelope **amlen** (amlenni)
every **pob**
everybody **pawb**
everything **i gyd**
everything **popeth**
expand (to) **ehangu**
expensive **drud**
explain (to) **egluro**
eye **llygad** (llygaid)

face **wyneb** (wynebau)
fact **ffaith** (ffeithiau)
factory **ffatri** (ffatrïoedd)
fail (to) **methu**
fair **ffair** (ffeiriau)
fair **teg**
faith **ffydd**
fall (to) **cwympo**
family **teulu** (teuluoedd)

famous **enwog**
fantastic **bendigedig**
far **pell**
farm **fferm:ffarm** (ffermydd)
farm (to) **ffermio:ffarmio**
farmer **ffermwr:ffarmwr**
  (ffermwyr)
fashionable **ffasiynol**
fast **cyflym**
fat **tew**
father **tad** (tadau)
fault **bai** (beiau)
fear **ofn** (ofnau)
February **Chwefror,**
  mis Chwefror
feel (to) **teimlo**
fence **ffens** (ffensys)
few **ychydig**
field **cae** (caeau)
field **maes** (meysydd)
fight (to) **ymladd**
figure **rhif** (rhifau)
fill (to) **llanw; llenwi**
film **ffilm** (ffilmiau)
finger **bys** (bysedd)
finish (to) **gorffen**
fire **tân** (tanau)
first **cyntaf**
fish **pysgodyn** (pysgod)
fish (to) **pysgota**
fit (to) **ffitio**
flame **fflam** (fflamau)
flash (to) **fflachio**
floor **llawr** (lloriau)

flower **blodyn** (blodau)
fly (to) **hedfan**
foam **ewyn**
fog **niwl** (niwloedd)
follow (to) **dilyn**
food **bwyd** (bwydydd)
fool **twpsyn**
foot **troed** (traed)
football **pêl-droed**
forget (to) **anghofio**
fork **fforc** (ffyrc)
forward **ymlaen**
free **rhydd**
fresh **ffres**
friend **cyfaill** (cyfeillion);
    ffrind (ffrindiau)
frock **ffrog** (ffrogiau)
from **o** TM; **wrth** TM
front **blaen** (blaenau)
frost **rhew**
fruit **ffrwyth** (ffrwythau)
full **llawn**
fun **hwyl**
funny **doniol**

game **gêm** (gemau: gêmau)
garage **garej**
garden **gardd** (gerddi)
gate **clwyd** (clwydi)
get better (to) **gwella**
gift **anrheg** (anrhegion)
girl **merch** (merched)
go (to) **mynd**
goal **gôl** (goliau)

God **Duw**
good **da**[1]
government **llywodraeth**
    (llywodraethau)
grandfather **taid** (teidiau)
    (North Wales form)
grandfather **tad-cu** (tadau-cu)
    (South Wales form)
grandmother **mam-gu**
    (mamau-cu) (South Wales
    form)
grandmother **nain** (neiniau)
    (North Wales form)
grass **porfa** (porfeydd)
green **gwyrdd**
grey **llwyd**
group **grŵp** (grwpiau)
grow (to) **tyfu**
hailstones **cesair**
hair **blewyn** (blew); **gwallt**
half **hanner** (haneri)
hall **neuadd** (neuaddau)
hammer **morthwyl**
    (morthwylion)
hand **llaw** (dwylo)
handsome **hardd**
happen (to) **digwydd**
happy **hapus**
hard **caled**
harp **telyn** (telynau)
hat **het** (hetiau)
have (to) **cael**
have to (to) **gorfod**
head **pen** (pennau)

healthy **iach**
hear (to) **clywed**
heart **calon** (calonnau)
heavy **trwm**
hell **uffern** (uffernau)
help **help**
help (to) **helpu**
hen **iâr** (ieir)
her **ei** TLl, H
here **yma**
here is/are **dyma** TM
hesitate (to) **petruso**
hide (to) **cuddio**
high **uchel**
hill **rhiw** (rhiwiau)
his **ei** TM
history **hanes**
hit (to) **bwrw**
hole **twll** (tyllau)
holidays **gwyliau**
home **cartref** (cartrefi)
honey **mêl**
hope (to) **gobeithio**
horse **ceffyl** (ceffylau)
hospital **ysbyty** (ysbytai)
hot **poeth; twym**
hour **awr** (oriau)
house **tŷ** (tai)
how **sut**
hurry (to) **brysio**
husband **gŵr** (gwŷr)
hymn **emyn** (emynau)

ice **iâ**
idea **syniad** (syniadau)
if **os**
ill **sâl**
important **pwysig**
in **mewn**
in **yn** TT
interesting **diddorol; difyr**
Internet **rhyngrwyd**
iron **haearn**
iron (to) **smwddio**
island **ynys** (ynysoedd)

jam **jam** (jamiau)
January **Ionawr, mis Ionawr**
jar **jar** (jariau)
jeans **jîns**
jelly **jeli** (jelis)
joke **jôc** (jôcs)
journey **taith** (teithiau)
jug **jwg** (jygiau)
July **Gorffennaf,**
   mis Gorffennaf
jump (to) **neidio**
June **Mehefin, mis Mehefin**

karate **karate**
keep (to) **cadw**
kettle **tegell** (tegellau)
key **agoriad** (agoriadau);
   allwedd (allweddau)
kick (to) **cicio**
kill (to) **lladd**
kind **caredig**

king **brenin** (brenhinoedd)
kitchen cegin (ceginau)
knee **glin** (gliniau)
knife **cyllell** (cyllyll)
know (to) **gwybod**

ladder ysgol² (ysgolion)
lake **llyn** (llynnoedd)
lamb **oen** (ŵyn)
lamp **lamp** (lampiau)
land **tir** (tiroedd)
language iaith (ieithoedd)
last night **neithiwr**
late hwyr
laugh (to) **chwerthin**
lavatory **tŷ bach**
lazy **diog**
lead (to) **arwain**
learn (to) **dysgu**
learner **dysgwr** (dysgwyr)
leave (to) **gadael**
leek cenhinen (cennin)
left **chwith**
leg coes (coesau)
lesson gwers (gwersi)
letter **llythyr** (llythyrau)
letter **llythyren** (llythrennau)
library **llyfrgell** (llyfrgelloedd)
lie **celwydd** (celwyddau)
lie (to) **gorwedd**
lift (to) **codi**
light **golau** (goleuadau)
light **ysgafn**
lightning **mellt**

like **fel**
like (to) **hoffi**
like tebyg
line **llinell** (llinellau)
lip gwefus (gwefusau)
listen (to) **gwrando**
live (to) **byw**
loaf torth (torthau)
lock **clo** (cloeon)
lock (to) **cloi**
lollipop **lolipop**
lonely unig
long hir
look (to) **edrych**
lorry **lorri** (lorïau)
lose (to) **colli**
loud **uchel**
love (to) **caru**
low isel
lucky lwcus

mail **post**
man **dyn** (dynion); **gŵr**
   (gwŷr)
many **llawer**
map **map** (mapiau)
March **Mawrth, mis Mawrth**
mark **marc** (marciau)
mark (to) **marcio**
market **marchnad**
   (marchnadoedd)
marry (to) **priodi**
mat **mat** (matiau)
May **Mai, mis Mai**

78

meal **pryd** (prydau)
meaning **ystyr** (ystyron)
measure (to) **mesur**
meeting **cyfarfod** (cyfarfodydd)
melt (to) **toddi**
memory **cof** (cofion)
merry **llawen**
message **neges** (negeseuon)
metal **metel** (metelau)
middle **canol**
mile **milltir** (milltiroedd)
milk **llefrith** (North Wales form)
milk **llaeth** (South Wales form)
minister **gweinidog** (gweinidogion)
minute **munud** (munudau)
mistake **camgymeriad** (camgymeriadau)
mix (to) **cymysgu**
money **arian**
monotonous **undonog**
month **mis** (misoedd)
moon **lleuad** (lleuadau)
more **mwy**
morning **bore**
mother **mam** (mamau)
mountain **mynydd** (mynyddoedd)
mouse **llygoden** (llygod)
mouth **ceg** (cegau)
move (to) **symud**
must **rhaid**
my **fy** TT

name **enw** (enwau)
narrow **cul**
nasty **cas**
natural **naturiol**
neat **twt**
nephew **nai** (neiaint)
nest **nyth** (nythod)
never **byth**
new **newydd**
news **newyddion**
nice **hyfryd**
niece **nith** (nithoedd)
night **nos:noswaith** (nosweithiau)
nobody/no one **neb**
noise **sŵn** (synau)
north **gogledd**
nose **trwyn** (trwynau)
nostalgia **hiraeth**
note **nodyn** (nodau)
nothing **dim**
notice (to) **sylwi**
November **Tachwedd, mis Tachwedd**
now **nawr**
number **rhif** (rhifau)
nurse **nyrs** (nyrsys)

obey (to) **ufuddhau**
oblong **petryal** (petryalau)
October **Hydref, mis Hydref**
odd **od**
office **swyddfa** (swyddfeydd)
oil **olew**

old **hen**
onion **winwnsyn** (winwns) (South Wales form)
onion **wnionyn** (wynionod: wynwyn) (North Wales form)
open (to) **agor**
orange (colour) **oren**[1]
orange (fruit) **oren**[2] (orenau)
other **llall** (lleill)
our **ein**
oven **ffwrn** (ffyrnau)
over **dros** TM

pack (to) **pacio**
pain **poen** (poenau)
painful **poenus**
paint **paent** (paentiau)
paint (to) **peintio**
paper **papur** (papurau)
parcel **parsel** (parseli)
parent **rhiant** (rhieni)
parliament **senedd** (seneddau)
part **rhan** (rhannau)
party **parti** (partïon)
pay (to) **talu**
pencil **pensil** (pensiliau)
penny **ceiniog** (ceiniogau)
people **pobl** (pobloedd)
perfect **perffaith**
perhaps **efallai**
perspire (to) **chwysu**
petrol **petrol**
phone **ffôn** (ffonau)

phone (to) **ffonio**
pianist **pianydd** (pianyddion)
piano **piano** (pianos)
pick (to) **pigo**
picnic **picnic**
picture **darlun** (darluniau); **llun** (lluniau)
piece **darn** (darnau)
pig **mochyn** (moch)
pink **pinc**
pipe **pibell** (pibellau)
pit **pwll** (pyllau)
pity **trueni**
place **lle** (lleoedd:llefydd)
plain **plaen**
plant (to) **plannu**
play (to) **chwarae**
player **chwaraewr** (chwaraewyr)
pleasure **pleser** (pleserau)
police force **heddlu** (heddluoedd)
policeman **heddwas** (heddweision)
pool **pwll** (pyllau)
poor **gwael**
poor **tlawd**
porridge **uwd**
possible **posibl**
potato **taten** (tatws)
pound **punt** (punnoedd: punnau)
practise (to) **ymarfer**
praise (to) **canmol**

prayer **gweddi** (gweddïau)
prepare (to) **paratoi**
present (gift) **anrheg** (anrhegion)
pretty **pert**
pretty **del** (North Wales form)
price **pris** (prisiau)
priest **offeiriad** (offeiriaid)
private **preifat**
prize **gwobr** (gwobrau)
problem **problem** (problemau)
professor **athro**
programme/program **rhaglen** (rhaglenni)
promise (to) **addo**
public house **tafarn** (tafarnau)
pull (to) **tynnu**
pyjamas **pyjamas**

quarrel (to) **ffraeo**
quiet **tawel**

race **ras** (rasys)
race (to) **rasio**
radio **radio**
raffle **raffl** (rafflau)
railway **rheilffordd** (rheilffyrdd)
rain (to) **bwrw glaw**
rain **glaw** (glawogydd)
rainbow **enfys** (enfysau)
rally **rali** (ralïau)
read (to) **darllen**
reason **rheswm** (rhesymau)

recipe **rysáit** (ryseitiau)
red **coch**
refuse (to) **gwrthod; pallu**
remember (to) **cofio**
reply (to) **ateb**
rescue (to) **achub**
right **de²**
right **iawn**
ring **modrwy** (modrwyau)
river **afon** (afonydd)
road **ffordd** (ffyrdd)
rock **craig** (creigiau)
rocket **roced** (rocedi)
roof **to** (toeau)
room **ystafell** (ystafelloedd)
rope **rhaff** (rhaffau)
rose **rhosyn** (rhosynnau)
row **rhes** (rhesi)
row (to) **rhwyfo**
rubbish **sbwriel**
rugby **rygbi**
rule **rheol** (rheolau)
run (to) **rhedeg**
runner **rhedwr** (rhedwyr)
rush (to) **rhuthro**

sad **trist**
saint **sant** (saint:seintiau)
salt **halen**
sand **tywod**
satisfied **bodlon**
saucepan **sosban** (sosbannau: sosbenni)
saucer **soser** (soseri)

save (to) **achub**
saw **llif** (llifiau)
say (to) **dweud**
school **ysgol**[1] (ysgolion)
science **gwyddoniaeth**
scissors **siswrn** (sisyrnau)
score **sgôr** (sgorau)
scratch (to) **crafu**
sea **môr** (moroedd)
search (to) **chwilio**
season **tymor** (tymhorau)
seat **sedd** (seddau:seddi)
second **ail**
second **eiliad** (eiliadau)
secret **cyfrinach** (cyfrinachau)
see (to) **gweld**
sell (to) **gwerthu**
send (to) **anfon**
September **Medi, mis Medi**
serious **difrifol**
shampoo **siampŵ** (siampŵau)
sharp **siarp**
shave (to) **siafio**
sheep **dafad** (defaid)
shine (to) **disgleirio**
ship **llong** (llongau)
shirt **crys** (crysau)
shock **sioc** (siociau)
shoe **esgid** (esgidiau)
shoot (to) **saethu**
shop **siop** (siopau)
short **byr**
shoulder **ysgwydd** (ysgwyddau)
shout (to) **gweiddi**

shovel **rhaw** (rhofiau)
show (to) **dangos**
show **sioe** (sioeau)
shut (to) **cau**
shy **swil**
side **ochr** (ochrau)
silver **arian**
simple **syml**
sing (to) **canu**
sister **chwaer** (chwiorydd)
sit (to) **eistedd**
ski (to) **sgio**
skip (to) **sgipio**
skirt **sgert** (sgertiau)
sky **awyr**
sleep (to) **cysgu**
slow **araf**
small **bach**
smoke **mwg**
smoke (to) **ysmygu**
snake **neidr** (nadredd: nadroedd)
snow **eira**
soap **sebon** (sebonau)
soccer **pêl-droed**
sock **hosan** (hosanau:sanau)
soft **meddal**
soldier **milwr** (milwyr)
some **rhai**
somebody/someone **rhywun** (rhywrai)
something **rhywbeth** (rhyw bethau)
sometimes **weithiau**

son **mab** (meibion)
sore **tost**
sour **sur**
south **de**[1]
speak (to) **siarad**
spectacles **sbectol** (sbectolau)
spend (to) **gwario**
spoon **llwy** (llwyau)
spring **gwanwyn** (gwanwynau)
square **sgwâr** (sgwariau)
squeeze (to) **gwasgu**
stage **llwyfan** (llwyfannau)
stairs **grisiau**
stamp **stamp** (stampiau)
stand (to) **sefyll**
star **seren** (sêr)
start (to) **dechrau**
station **gorsaf** (gorsafoedd)
stick **ffon** (ffyn)
stocking **hosan** (hosanau: sanau)
stomach **stumog** (stumogau);
   bol:bola
stone **carreg** (cerrig)
storm **storm** (stormydd)
story **stori** (straeon)
straight **syth**
strange **rhyfedd**
stream **nant** (nentydd)
street **stryd** (strydoedd)
strength **nerth**
strong **cryf**
student **myfyriwr** (myfyrwyr)
succeed (to) **llwyddo**
sugar **siwgr** (siwgrau)

summer **haf** (hafau)
sun **haul** (heuliau)
supper **swper** (swperau)
swallow (to) **llyncu**
swan **alarch** (elyrch)
sweet **melys**
sweets **losin**
swim (to) **nofio**

table **bwrdd** (byrddau)
take (to) **cymryd**
tale **chwedl** (chwedlau)
tall **tal**
tap **tap** (tapiau)
tasty **blasus**
tea **te**
teacher (female) **athrawes**
   (athrawesau)
teacher (male) **athro** (athrawon)
team **tîm** (timau:timoedd)
television **teledu**
tennis **tennis**
tent **pabell** (pebyll)
term **tymor** (tymhorau)
text (to) **tecstio**
thank (to) **diolch**
that **a**[2]
theatre **theatr** (theatrau)
their **eu** H
theme **thema** (themâu)
there is/are **dacw** TM
there is/are **dyna** TM
thermometer **thermomedr**
   (thermomedrau)

83

thief **lleidr** (lladron)
thin **tenau**
thing **peth** (pethau)
think (to) **meddwl**
through **trwy** TM
throw (to) **taflu**
thumb **bawd** (bodiau)
thunder **taran** (taranau)
ticket **tocyn** (tocynnau)
tidy **taclus**
tie (to) **clymu**
tight **tyn**
time **amser** (amserau)
tin **tun** (tuniau)
tire (to) **blino**
to **i** TM; **at** TM
today **heddiw**
toe **bys** (bysedd)
toilet **toiled** (toiledau)
tomorrow **yfory**
tongue **tafod** (tafodau)
tonight **heno**
too **rhy** TM; **hefyd**
too much **gormod**
tooth **dant** (dannedd)
towel **tywel** (tywelion)
town **tref** (trefi:trefydd)
toy **tegan** (teganau)
train **trên** (trenau)
treasure **trysor** (trysorau)
tree **coeden** (coed)
trip (to) **baglu**
trip **trip** (tripiau)

trousers **trywser:trywsus**
 (trywserau:trywsusau)
true **gwir**
truth **gwirionedd**
 (gwirioneddau)
turn (to) **troi**
tyre **teiar** (teiars)

ugly **hyll**
uncle **ewythr:ewyrth**
 (ewythredd:ewythrod)
under **dan** TM
under **o dan** TM
under **tan** TM
understand (to) **deall**
undo (to) **agor**
union **undeb** (undebau)
university **prifysgol**
 (prifysgolion)
untidy **blêr**
upstairs **llofft** (llofftydd)
use (to) **defnyddio**

van **fan** (faniau)
verse **pennill** (penillion)
vicar **ficer** (ficeriaid)
village **pentref** (pentrefi)
vinegar **finegr**
violin **feiolin** (feiolinau)
voice **llais** (lleisiau)

wait (to) **aros**
wake (to) **deffro; dihuno**
Wales **Cymru**

walk (to) **cerdded**
walking stick **ffon** (ffyn)
wall **mur** (muriau); **wal** (waliau)
want **eisiau**
war **rhyfel** (rhyfeloedd)
warm **cynnes**
wash (to) **golchi**
watch **watsh** (watshys)
watch (to) **gwylio**
water **dŵr** (dyfroedd)
wave (to) **chwifio**
wave **ton** (tonnau)
weak **gwan**
wear (to) **gwisgo**
weather **tywydd**
wedding **priodas** (priodasau)
weeds **chwyn**
week **wythnos** (wythnosau)
Welsh **Cymreig**
Welsh (language) **Cymraeg**
Welshman **Cymro** (Cymry)
Welshwoman **Cymraes**
west **gorllewin**
wet **gwlyb**
wheel **olwyn** (olwynion)
when **pan** TM
whisker **blewyn**
whistle (to) **chwibanu**
white **gwyn**
who **a**[2]
who? **a**
why **pam**
wide **llydan**
wife **gwraig** (gwragedd)

wild **gwyllt**
will[1] (as in willpower) **ewyllys**
will[2] (bequest) **ewyllys**
   (ewyllysiau)
win (to) **ennill**
wind **gwynt** (gwyntoedd)
window **ffenestr** (ffenestri)
winter **gaeaf** (gaeafau)
wipe (to) **sychu**
with **â**[1] TLI; **ag**
with **gyda** TLI
without **heb** TM
woman **gwraig** (gwragedd);
   menyw (menywod)
wonder **rhyfeddod**
   (rhyfeddodau)
wood **pren** (prennau)
wool **gwlân**
word **gair** (geiriau)
work **gwaith** (gweithiau)
work (to) **gweithio**
worker **gweithiwr** (gweithwyr)
World Wide Web **Gwe**
   Fyd-eang
wrist **garddwrn:arddwrn**
   (garddyrnau:arddyrnau)
write (to) **ysgrifennu**

yellow **melyn**
yesterday **ddoe**
young **ifanc**
your **dy** TM
your **eich**

Y Geiriadur (Welsh–English)

The Welsh alphabet

a b c **ch** d **dd** e f **ff** g **ng** h i j l **ll** m n o p **ph** r **rh** s t **th** u w y

\|/
The single letters of the alphabet follow the same order as the English alphabet. However, the Welsh 'double' letters are in fact <u>separate letters in their own right</u> which <u>follow the initial single letter</u> (except in the case of **ng**).

The following letters indicate the mutation triggered by the word:

TM   Treiglad Meddal   TT   Treiglad Trwynol
TLl   Treiglad Llaes   H   H before a vowel

The colour code

enw = noun masculine *bachgen*
enw = **noun feminine** *merch*
enw = **noun plural** *newyddion*
enw = **noun masculine**
or noun feminine
(depending on North Wales or South Wales, e.g. **munud**; or on the gender, e.g. **nyrs** (male or female), though this is rare.)
ansoddair = adjective *bach*
berfenw = verb-noun *canu*

so!

annwyd = *a* cold   **oer** = cold
diod = *a* drink   **yfed** = *to* drink
marc = *a* mark   **marcio** = *to* mark
newydd = new   **newyddion** = news

86

A

a¹ and TLI
a² that, who TM
â¹ with TLI
â² as TLI
ac and
actio to act
achub to rescue, to save
adeiladu to build, to construct
aderyn (adar) bird
adio to add
addo to promise
afal (afalau) apple
afon (afonydd) river
ag with
agor to open, to undo
agoriad (agoriadau) key
angel (angylion) angel
anghofio to forget
angor (angorau) anchor
ail second
alarch (elyrch) swan
allwedd (allweddau) key
am at, about TM
ambiwlans (ambiwlansys) ambulance
amlen (amlenni) envelope
amser (amserau) time
anfon to send
anifail (anifeiliaid) animal
annwyd (anwydau) cold
anodd difficult
anrheg (anrhegion) gift, present

ar at, about TM
araf slow
arian money, silver
aros to wait
arwain to lead
asgwrn (esgyrn) bone
at to TM
ateb (atebion) answer
ateb to answer, to reply
athrawes (athrawesau) teacher
athro (athrawon) teacher, professor
awr (oriau) hour
Awst August
awyr sky
awyren (awyrennau) aeroplane

B

babi (babis) baby
bach small
bachgen (bechgyn) boy
bag (bagiau) bag
baglu to trip
bai (beiau) blame, fault
balŵn (balwnau) balloon
banana (bananas) banana
bara bread
basged (basgedi) basket
bat (batiau) bat
bàth (bathiau) bath
baw dirt, grime
bawd (bodiau) thumb, big toe

beic (beiciau) bike
belt (beltiau) belt
bendigedig fantastic
berwi to boil
blaen (blaenau) front
blanced (blancedi) blanket
blasus tasty
blêr untidy
blewyn (blew) hair, whisker
blino to tire
blodyn (blodau) flower
bocs (bocsys) box
boch (bochau) cheek
bodlon satisfied
boddi to drown
bol:bola (boliau) belly, stomach
bore morning
braich (breichiau) arm
brecwast (brecwastau) breakfast
brenin (brenhinoedd) king
brown brown
brwnt dirty
brwsio to brush
brysio to hurry
budr dirty
buwch (buchod) cow
bwrdd (byrddau) table, board
bwrw to hit
bwrw glaw to rain
bwyd (bwydydd) food
bwyta to eat
byr short
bys (bysedd) finger, toe

byth never
byw to live

C

cacen (cacennau) cake
cadair (cadeiriau) chair
cadw to keep
cae (caeau) field
cael to have
caffi (caffis) café
caled hard
calon (calonnau) heart
camera (camerâu) camera
camgymeriad (camgymeriadau) mistake
canmol to praise
cannwyll (canhwyllau) candle
canol middle
canu to sing
cap (capiau) cap
capel (capeli) chapel
car (ceir) car
caredig kind
cario to carry
carreg (cerrig) stone
cartref (cartrefi) home
caru to love
cas nasty
castell (cestyll) castle
cath (cathod) cat
cau to shut
caws cheese
cefn (cefnau) back

ceffyl (ceffylau) horse
ceg (cegau) mouth
cegin (ceginau) kitchen
ceiniog (ceiniogau) penny
celwydd (celwyddau) lie
cenhinen (cennin) leek
cenhinen Bedr (cennin Pedr)
   daffodil
cerdded to walk
cesair hailstones
ci (cŵn) dog
cicio to kick
cinio (ciniawau) dinner
clapio to clap
clo (cloeon) lock
cloc (clociau) clock
cloch (clychau) bell
cloi to lock
clust (clustiau) ear
clustog (clustogau) cushion
clwyd (clwydi) gate
clymu to tie
clywed to hear
cnoi to bite
coch red
codi to lift
coeden (coed) tree
coes (coesau) leg
cof (cofion) memory
cofio to remember
coffi coffee
colli to lose
côr (corau) choir
cors (corsydd) bog

cot:côt (cotiau) coat
crafu to scratch
craig (creigiau) rock
credu to believe
crio to cry
cryf strong
crys (crysau) shirt
cuddio to hide
cul narrow
cwch (cychod) boat
cwmwl (cymylau) cloud
cwpan (cwpanau) cup
cwpwrdd (cypyrddau)
   cupboard
cwrw beer
cwympo to fall
cyfaill (cyfeillion) friend
cyfarfod (cyfarfodydd)
   meeting
cyflym fast
cyfrifiadur (cyfrifiaduron)
   computer
cyfrinach (cyfrinachau)
   a secret
cyfforddus comfortable
cylch (cylchoedd) circle
cyllell (cyllyll) knife
Cymraeg Welsh (language)
Cymraes Welshwoman
Cymreig Welsh
Cymro (Cymry) Welshman
Cymru Wales
cymryd to take
cymysgu to mix

cyn¹ before
cyn² as TM
cynnar early
cynnes warm
cyntaf first
cysgu to sleep
cytuno to agree

Ch
chwaer (chwiorydd) sister
chwarae to play
chwaraewr (chwaraewyr) player
chwedl (chwedlau) tale
Chwefror February
chwerthin to laugh
chwibanu to whistle
chwifio to wave
chwilio to search
chwith left
chwyn weeds
chwysu to perspire
chwythu to blow

D
da¹ good
da² cattle
dacw there is/are TM
daear¹ earth
Daear² planet Earth
dafad (defaid) sheep
dal to catch
dan under TM
dangos to show

dant (dannedd) tooth
darganfod to discover
darlun (darluniau) picture
darllen to read
darn (darnau) piece
dathlu to celebrate
dawnsio to dance
de¹ south
de² right
deall to understand
dechrau to begin, to start
defnyddio to use
deffro to wake
del pretty (North Wales form)
derbyn to accept
desg (desgiau) desk
dewis to choose
dewr brave
diddorol interesting
diflas boring
difrifol serious
difyr interesting
dig angry
digio to become angry
digon enough
digwydd to happen
dihuno to wake
dilyn to follow
dillad clothes
dim nothing
dinas (dinasoedd) city
diod (diodydd) drink
diog lazy
diolch to thank

disglair bright
disgleirio to shine
diwedd end
diwrnod (diwrnodau) day
doctor (doctoriaid) doctor
dod to come
doniol funny
dosbarth (dosbarthiadau) class
draig (dreigiau) dragon
dringo to climb
dros over TM
drud expensive
drwg bad
drws (drysau) door
du black
Duw God
dweud to say
dwfn deep
dŵr (dyfroedd) water
dwyrain east
dy your TM
dydd (dyddiau) day
　dydd Sul Sunday
　dydd Llun Monday
　dydd Mawrth Tuesday
　dydd Mercher Wednesday
　dydd Iau Thursday
　dydd Gwener Friday
　dydd Sadwrn Saturday
dyma here is/are TM
dyn (dynion) man
dyna there is/are TM
dysgu to learn
dysgwr (dysgwyr) learner

Dd
ddoe yesterday

E
e-bost (e-byst) email
Ebrill April
edmygu to admire
edrych to look
efallai perhaps
egluro to explain
eglwys (eglwysi) church
egni energy
ehangu to expand
ei her TLI, H; his TM
eich your
eiliad (eiliadau) second
ein our H
eira snow
eisiau want
eistedd to sit
eisteddfod (eisteddfodau)
e-lyfr (e-lyfrau) e-book
emyn (emynau) hymn
enfys (enfysau) rainbow
ennill to win
enw (enwau) name
enwog famous
esgid (esgidiau) shoe
eto again
etholiad (etholiadau) election
eu their H
ewyllys[1] will (as in willpower)
ewyllys[2] (ewyllysiau) will
　(bequest)

ewyn foam
ewythr:ewyrth (ewythredd: ewythrod) uncle

F
fan (faniau) van
feiolin (feiolinau) violin
fel like
ficer (ficeriaid) vicar
finegr vinegar
fy my TT

Ff
ffair (ffeiriau) fair
ffaith (ffeithiau) fact
ffasiynol fashionable
ffatri (ffatrïoedd) factory
ffenestr (ffenestri) window
ffens (ffensys) fence
fferm:ffarm (ffermydd) farm
ffermio:ffarmio to farm
ffermwr:ffarmwr (ffermwyr) farmer
ffilm (ffilmiau) film
ffitio to fit
fflachio to flare, to flash
fflam (fflamau) flame
ffon (ffyn) stick; walking stick
ffôn (ffonau) phone
ffonio to phone
fforc (ffyrc) fork
ffordd (ffyrdd) road
ffraeo to quarrel
ffres fresh

ffrind (ffrindiau) friend
ffrog (ffrogiau) frock
ffrwyth (ffrwythau) fruit
ffwrn (ffyrnau) oven
ffydd faith

G
gadael to leave
gaeaf (gaeafau) winter
gair (geiriau) word
galw to call
gallu to be able to
gan by TM
gardd (gerddi) garden
garddwrn:arddwrn (garddyrnau:arddyrnau) wrist
garej garage
geiriadur (geiriaduron) dictionary
gêm (gemau: gêmau) game
geni to give birth to
glân clean
glan (glannau) side, bank
glas blue
glaw (glawogydd) rain
glin (gliniau) knee
glo coal
gobeithio to hope
gof (gofaint) blacksmith
gofalus careful
gofyn to ask
gogledd north
gôl (goliau) goal

golau (goleuadau) light
golchi to wash
gorau best
gorfod to have to
gorffen to finish
Gorffennaf July
gorllewin west
gormod too much
gorsaf (gorsafoedd) station
gorwedd to lie
grisiau stairs
grŵp (grwpiau) group
gwaed blood
gwael poor, shoddy
gwaelod (gwaelodion) bottom
gwag empty
gwahanol different
gwaith (gweithiau) work
gwallt (gwalltiau) hair
gwan weak
gwanwyn (gwanwynau) spring
gwario to spend
gwasgu to squeeze
gweddi (gweddïau) prayer
gwefus (gwefusau) lip
Gwe Fyd-eang World Wide Web
gweiddi to shout
gweinidog (gweinidogion) minister
gweithio to work
gweithiwr (gweithwyr) worker

gweld to see
gwely (gwelyau:gwelâu) bed
gwell better
gwella to get better
gwers (gwersi) lesson
gwerthu to sell
gwir true
gwiroinedd truth
gwisgo to dress, to wear
gwlad (gwledydd) country
gwlân wool
gwlyb wet
gwneud to do
gwobr (gwobrau) prize
gŵr (gwŷr) husband, man
gwraig (gwragedd) wife, woman
gwrando to listen
gwrthod to refuse
gwybod to know
gwyddoniaeth science
gwyliau holidays
gwylio to watch
gwyllt wild
gwyn white
gwynt wind
gwyrdd green
gyda with TLl
gyrru to drive

H
haearn (haearnau) iron
haf (hafau) summer
halen salt

93

hanes history, account
hanner (haneri) half
hapus happy
hardd handsome
haul (heuliau) sun
hawdd easy
heb without TM
hedfan to fly
heddiw today
heddlu (heddluoedd) police force
heddwas (heddweision) policeman
hefyd also; too
help help
helpu to help
hen old
heno tonight
het (hetiau) hat
hir long
hiraeth nostalgia
hoffi to like
hosan (hosanau:sanau) sock, stocking
hufen cream
hwyl (hwyliau) fun
hwyr late
hydref (hydrefau) autumn
Hydref October
hyfryd nice
hyll ugly

I
i to TM

iâ ice
iach healthy
iaith (ieithoedd) language
iâr (ieir) hen
iawn right
ifanc young
i gyd all, everything
injan (injans) engine
Ionawr January
isel low

J
jam (jamiau) jam
jar (jariau) jar
jeli (jelis) jelly
jîns jeans
jôc (jôcs) joke
jwg (jygiau) jug

K
karate karate

L
lamp (lampiau) lamp
lawr:i lawr down
lolipop lollipop
lorri (lorïau) lorry
losin sweet, sweets
lwcus lucky

Ll
lladd to kill, to slaughter, to slay
llaeth milk (South Wales form)

llais (lleisiau) voice
llall (lleill) other
llanw to fill
llaw (dwylo) hand
llawen merry
llawer many
llawn full
llawr (lloriau) floor
lle (lleoedd:llefydd) place
llefain to cry
llefrith milk (North Wales form)
lleidr (lladron) thief
llenwi to fill
llestri dishes
lleuad (lleuadau) moon
llif (llifiau) saw
llinell (llinellau) line
lliw (lliwiau) colour
Lloegr England
llofft (llofftydd) upstairs
llong (llongau) ship
llosgi to burn
llun (lluniau) photograph, picture
llwy (llwyau) spoon
llwyd grey
llwyddo to succeed
llwyfan (llwyfannau) stage
llydan broad, wide
llyfr (llyfrau) book
llyfrgell (llyfrgelloedd) library
llygad (llygaid) eye
llygoden (llygod) mouse

llyn (llynnoedd) lake
llyncu to swallow
llys (llysoedd) court
llythyr (llythyrau) letter
llythyren (llythrennau) letter
llywodraeth (llywodraethau) government

M
mab (meibion) son
maes (meysydd) field
Mai May
mam (mamau) mother
mam-gu (mamau-cu) grandmother (South Wales form)
map (mapiau) map
marc (marciau) mark
marcio to mark
marchnad (marchnadoedd) market
marw to die
mat (matiau) mat
mawr big
Mawrth March
Medi September
meddal soft
meddwl to think
meddyg (meddygon) doctor
Mehefin June
mêl honey
melyn yellow
melys sweet
mellt lightning

menyn butter
menyw (menywod) woman
merch (merched) girl, daughter
mesur to measure
metel (metelau) metal
methu to fail
mewn in
milwr (milwyr) soldier
milltir (milltiroedd) mile
mis (misoedd) month
   mis Ionawr January
   mis Chwefror February
   mis Mawrth March
   mis Ebrill April
   mis Mai May
   mis Mehefin June
   mis Gorffennaf July
   mis Awst August
   mis Medi September
   mis Hydref October
   mis Tachwedd November
   mis Rhagfyr December
mochyn (moch) pig
modrwy (modrwyau) ring
modryb (modrybedd) aunt
môr (moroedd) sea
morthwyl (morthwylion) hammer
munud (munudau) minute
mur (muriau) wall
mwg smoke
mwy bigger, more
mwynhau (to) enjoy
myfyriwr (myfyrwyr) student

mynd to go
mynydd (mynyddoedd) mountain

N
Nadolig (Nadoligau) Christmas
nai (neiaint) nephew
nain (neiniau) grandmother (North Wales form)
nant (nentydd) brook, stream
naturiol natural
nawr now
neb nobody, no one
neges (negeseuon) message
neidio to jump
neidr (nadredd:nadroedd) snake
neithiwr last night
nerth strength
neuadd (neuaddau) hall
newid to change
newydd new
newyddion news
nith (nithoedd) niece
niwl (niwloedd) fog
nodyn (nodau) note
nofio (to) swim
nos:noswaith (nosweithiau) night
nyrs (nyrsys) nurse
nyth (nythod) nest

O

o from TM
ochr (ochrau) side
od eccentric, odd
o dan TM under
oed:oedran age
oedolyn (oedolion) adult
oen (ŵyn) lamb
oer cold
ofn (ofnau) fear, fright
ofnadwy awful
offeiriad (offeiriaid) priest
oherwydd because
olew oil
olwyn (olwynion) wheel
ond but
oren¹ (orenau) orange (fruit)
oren² orange (colour)
os if

P

pabell (pebyll) tent
pacio to pack
paent (paentiau) paint
palu to dig
pallu to refuse
pam why
pan when TM
papur (papurau) paper,
   newspaper
paratoi to prepare
parsel (parseli) parcel
parti (partïon) party
pawb everybody

peidio to cease
peintio to paint
pêl (peli) ball
pêl-droed football, soccer
pell far
pen (pennau) head
pen blwydd:pen-blwydd
   (pennau blwydd:
   penblwyddi) birthday
pennill (penillion) verse
penodi to appoint
pen-ôl (penolau) backside
pensil (pensiliau) pencil
pentref (pentrefi) village
perffaith perfect
pert pretty
peryglus dangerous
peswch cough
pesychu to cough
petrol petrol
petruso to hesitate
petryal (petryalau) oblong
peth (pethau) thing
piano (pianos) piano
pianydd (pianyddion) pianist
pibell (pibellau) pipe
picnic picnic
pigo to pick
pinc pink
plaen plain
plannu to plant
plentyn (plant) child
pleser (pleserau) pleasure
plygu to bend

pob every
pobi to bake
pobl (pobloedd) people
poen pain
poenus painful
poeth hot
pont (pontydd) bridge
popeth everything
porfa (porfeydd) grass
posibl possible
post mail, post
potel (poteli) bottle
preifat private
pren (prennau) wood
pridd (priddoedd) earth, soil
prifddinas (prifddinasoedd) capital city
prifysgol (prifysgolion) university
priodas (priodasau) wedding, marriage
priodi to marry
pris (prisiau) price
problem (problemau) problem
pryd (prydau) meal
prynhawn (prynhawniau) afternoon
prynu to buy
prysur busy
punt (punnoedd:punnau) pound
pwdin (pwdinau) dessert, pudding

pwll (pyllau) pool, pit
pwysig important
pyjamas pyjamas
pysgodyn (pysgod) fish
pysgota to fish

R

radio radio
raffl (rafflau) raffle
rali (raliau) rally
ras (rasys) race
rasio to race
roced (rocedi) rocket
rygbi rugby
rysáit (ryseitiau) recipe

Rh

rhad cheap
rhaff (rhaffau) rope
Rhagfyr December
rhaglen (rhaglenni) programme, program
rhai some
rhaid must
rhan (rhannau) part
rhannu to divide
rhaw (rhofiau) shovel
rhedeg to run
rhedwr (rhedwyr) runner
rheilffordd (rheilffyrdd) railway
rheol (rheolau) rule
rhes (rhesi) row
rheswm (rhesymau) reason

rhew frost, ice
rhiant (rhieni) parent
rhif (rhifau) figure, number
rhiw (rhiwiau) hill
rhosyn (rhosynnau) rose
rhuthro to rush
rhwng between
rhwydd easy
rhwyfo to row
rhy too TM
rhydd free
rhyfedd strange, weird
rhyfeddod (rhyfeddodau) wonder
rhyfeddol astonishing
rhyfeddu to be amazed
rhyfel (rhyfeloedd) war
rhyngrwyd Internet
rhywbeth (rhyw bethau) something
rhywun (rhywrai) somebody, someone

S

Saesneg English (language)
Saesnes (Saesnesau) Englishwoman
saethu to shoot
Sais (Saeson) Englishman
sâl ill
sant (saint:seintiau) saint
sbectol (sbectolau) glasses, spectacles
sbwriel rubbish

sebon (sebonau) soap
sedd (seddau:seddi) seat
sefyll to stand
seiclo to cycle
Seisnig English
senedd (seneddau) parliament, senate
seremoni (seremonïau) ceremony
seren (sêr) star
sgert (sgertiau) skirt
sgio to ski
sgipio to skip
sgôr (sgorau) score
sgwâr (sgwariau) square
siafio to shave
siampŵ (siampŵau) shampoo
sianel (sianeli:sianelau) channel
siarad to speak
siarp sharp
sigarét (sigaretau) cigarette
sioc (siociau) shock
siocled (siocledi) chocolate
sioe (sioeau) show
siop (siopau) shop
siswrn (sisyrnau) scissors
siwgr (siwgrau) sugar
smwddio to iron
sosban (sosbannau:sosbenni) saucepan
soser (soseri) saucer
stamp (stampiau) stamp
stori (straeon) story

storm (stormydd) storm
stryd (strydoedd) street
stumog (stumogau) stomach
sur sour
sut how
swil shy
swn (synau) noise
swper (swperau) supper
swyddfa (swyddfeydd) office
sych dry
sychu to dry, to wipe
sylwi to notice
syml simple
symud to move
syniad (syniadau) idea
syth straight

T
taclus neat, tidy
Tachwedd November
tad (tadau) father
tad-cu (tadau-cu) grandfather
  (South Wales form)
tafarn (tafarnau) pub, public
  house
taflu to throw
tafod (tafodau) tongue
taid (teidiau) grandfather
  (North Wales form)
taith (teithiau) journey
tal tall
talu to pay
tan under TM
tân (tanau) fire

tap (tapiau) tap
taran (taranau) thunder
taten (tatws) potato
tawel quiet
te tea
tebyg like
tecstio to text
teg fair
tegan (teganau) toy
tegell (tegellau) kettle
teiar (teiars) tyre
teimlo to feel
teisen (teisennau) cake
teledu television
telyn (telynau) harp
tenau thin
tennis tennis
teulu (teuluoedd) family
tew fat
tîm (timau:timoedd) team
tir (tiroedd) land
tlawd poor
to (toeau) roof
tocyn (tocynnau) ticket
toddi to melt
toiled (toiledau) toilet
ton (tonnau) wave
torf (torfeydd) crowd
torri to break
torth (torthau) loaf
tost sore, ill
traed feet
traeth (traethau) beach,
  sands

tref (trefi:trefydd) town
trên (trenau) train
trip (tripiau) trip
trist sad
troed (traed) foot
troi to turn
trueni pity
trwm heavy
trwy through TM
trwyn (trwynau) nose
trydan electricity
trysor (trysorau) treasure
trywser:trywsus
 (trywserau:trywsusau)
 trousers
tun (tuniau) tin
twll (tyllau) hole
twp daft
twpsyn fool
twt neat
twym hot
tŷ (tai) house
tŷ bach lavatory
tyfu to grow
tymor (tymhorau) season,
 term
tyn tight
tynnu to draw, to pull
tywel (tywelion) towel
tywod sand
tywydd weather
tywyll dark

Th
theatr (theatrau) theatre
thema (themâu) theme
thermomedr (thermomedrau)
 thermometer

U
uchel high, loud
ufuddhau to obey
uffern (uffernau) hell
undeb (undebau) union
undonog monotonous
unig only, lonely
unrhyw any
uwchben above
uwd porridge

W
wal (waliau) wall
watsh (watshys) watch
wedi after
wedyn after, afterwards
weithiau sometimes
winwnsyn (winwns) onion
 (South Wales form)
wrth from, by TM
wy (wyau) egg
wyneb (wynebau) face,
 surface
wynionyn
 (wynionod:wynwyn) onion
 (North Wales form)
wythnos (wythnosau) week

Y

ychydig few
yfed to drink
yfory tomorrow
yma here
ymarfer to practise,
  to exercise
ymddiheuro to apologize
ymennydd (ymenyddiau:
  ymenyddion) brain
ymladd to fight
ymlaen ahead, forward
yn at, in TT
ynys (ynysoedd) island
ysbyty (ysbytai) hospital
ysgafn light
ysgol[1] (ysgolion) school
ysgol[2] (ysgolion) ladder
ysgrifennu to write
ysgwydd (ysgwyddau)
  shoulder
ysmygu to smoke
ystafell (ystafelloedd) room
ystyr (ystyron) meaning

Appendix 1

The Little Words and the mutations they trigger

TM Treiglad Meddal   TT Treiglad Trwynol   TLl Treiglad Llaes

Welsh word	English equivalent	Part of speech	Treiglad
a	and	conjunction	TLl *ci a chath*
a	that, who	relative pronoun	TM *Y dyn a welodd y ci*
a	did?	interrogative particle	TM *A welaist ti'r bachgen?*
â	with	preposition	TLl *Y ferch â chot goch*
â	as	conjunction	TLl *mor goch â thân*
am	at, for	preposition	TM *am ddau o'r gloch*
ar	on	preposition	TM *ar gefn y ceffyl*
at	to	preposition	TM *ysgrifennu at gyfaill*
can	100	numeral	TT blwydd, blynedd, diwrnod; *can mlynedd*
cyn	as	adverbial particle	TM (except 'll' and 'rh'), *cyn goched â thân*
cyn	before	preposition	**none**
chwe	6	numeral	TLl *chwe chath*
dacw	there is/are	adverb	TM *Dacw gath*
dan	under	preposition	TM *afon yn llifo dan bont*
dau	2	numeral (masculine)	TM *dau gi*
deg	10	numeral	**none**
deng	10	numeral	TT blwydd, blynedd, diwrnod; TM *deng mlwydd, deng waith*

deuddeg	12	numeral	**none**
deuddeng	12	numeral	TT blwydd, blynedd, diwrnod; TM gwaith (*as with 'deng'*)
deunaw	18	numeral	TT blwydd, blynedd, diwrnod (*as with 'deuddeng'*)
dros	over	preposition	TM *mynd dros bont*
drwy	through	preposition	TM *mynd drwy ddŵr a thân*
dwy	2	numeral (feminine)	TM *dwy gath*
dy	your	personal pronoun	TM *dy lyfr*
dyma	here is/are	adverb	TM *dyma le da*
dyna	there is/are	adverb	TM *dyna le gwlyb*
ei (hi)	her	personal pronoun	1. TLI *ei chath* 2. Aspirate 'h' *ei hysgol*
ei (ef)	his	personal pronoun	TM *ei law*
eich	your	personal pronoun	**none**
ein	our	personal pronoun	Aspirate 'h' *ein hathro*
eithaf	quite	adverb	**none**
eu	their	personal pronoun	Aspirate 'h' *eu hathro*
fe		preverbal particle	TM *fe ddaeth yn gynnar*
fy	my	personal pronoun	TT *fy nhad*
gan	by	preposition	TM *cân gan ferch*
go	quite	adverb	TM *go dda*

gweddol	fairly	adverb	TM *gweddol dda*
gyda	with	preposition	TLI *eisteddodd gyda thad John*
hanner	half	noun	**none**
heb	without	preposition	TM *heb ddŵr*
hyd	until	preposition	TM *eisteddwch hyd ddiwedd y gân*
i	to	preposition	TM *mynd i Gaerdydd*
'i (hi)	her	personal pronoun	1. TLI *hi a'i thad* 2. Aspirate 'h' *hi a'i hathrawes*
'i (ef)	his	personal pronoun	TM *ef a'i fam*
'm	me	personal pronoun	Aspirate 'h' *y dyn a'm hanfonodd*
mi		preverbal particle	TM *'Mi welais jac-y-do'*
mor	as	adverb	TM **except** 'll', 'rh', *mor fawr, mor llwyd*
mwy	more	adjective	**none**
'n		adverbial 'yn'	TM **except** 'll', 'rh', *Mae'n dda; mae'n rhwydd*
na	nor	negative conjunction	TLI *ci na chath*
naw	9	numeral (cardinal)	TT *blwydd, blynedd, diwrnod; naw mlynedd*
neu	or	conjunction	TM (except verb forms) *adrodd neu ganu* **but** *adroddwch neu canwch*
o	from	preposition	TM *o Fangor*
os	if	interrogative particle	**none**

105

pa	which	interrogative pronoun	TM *pa lyfr*
pan	when	conjunction	TM *pan welodd*
pe	if	conjunction	**none**
pedair	4	numeral (feminine)	nouns **none**; TM feminine adjectives, *pedair fawr*
pob	every	adjective	**none**
prif	main, chief	adjective	TM *Prif Weinidog*
pum	5	numeral	TT *blwydd, blynedd, diwrnod; pum niwrnod* TM feminine adjectives *pum denau*
pwy	who, what	interrogative pronoun	TM *Pwy ddaeth i mewn?*
'r		the definite article	TM singular feminine nouns **except** 'll' and 'rh', *y bachgen a'r fuwch a'r rhaff*
rhy		adverb	TM *rhy dawel*
saith	7	numeral	TT *blwydd, blynedd, diwrnod; saith mlynedd*
sut	what sort; how	interrogative pronoun	TM nouns *sut ddyn oedd John*; berfau **none** *Sut daeth ef i mewn?*
tair	3	numeral (feminine)	nouns **none**; TM feminine adjectives, *tair bert*
tri	3	numeral (masculine)	TLI nouns, *tri chi*
tros			see **dros**
trwy			see drwy
tua	approximately	preposition	TLI *tua thair milltir*

'th	your	personal pronoun	TM *ti a'th frawd*
ugain	20	numeral	TT *blwydd, blynedd, diwrnod; ugain mlynedd*
un	1	numeral (feminine)	1. TM noun (except 'll' and 'rh') *un gath; un llong* 2. TM adjective (including 'll' a 'rh') *Mae'r afon yn un lydan* 3. TT *blwydd, blynedd* in compound numerals *Un mlynedd ar hugain*
'w (nhw)	their/them	personal pronoun	'h' Aspirate Mutation *Pwy sy'n mynd i'w hateb*
'w (ef)	his	personal pronoun	TM *Rwy'n mynd i'w dŷ*
'w (hi)	her	personal pronoun	1. TLl 2. 'h' Aspirate Mutation *Mae hi'n rhoi bwyd i'w chi*
wrth	against	preposition	TM *Arhosodd wrth ddrws y tŷ*
wyth	8	numeral	TT *blwydd, blynedd, diwrnod; wyth mlwydd oed*
y	the	definite article	TM feminine nouns except 'll' and 'rh', *y gath; y rhaff*
yn:ym:yng	in	preposition	TT *Yng Nghaernarfon*
yn		predicative and adverbial	TM (except 'll' and 'rh'), *yn ferch; yn llong; yn dda; yn llawen*
yn		before verb-noun	**none**
yr	the	definite article	TM some feminine nouns starting with **g**, *yr ardd*

For a fuller list of words that trigger mutation and the rules governing mutation see D. Geraint Lewis, *Y Treigladur: A Check-list of Welsh Mutations* (Gomer).

Appendix 2

Remember the gender

1. Pink nouns and **Blue nouns**
This draws on the imagination. All feminine nouns are printed in pink, all masculine nouns are printed in **blue.**

When learning a new word, depending on its gender, paint the most zany picture possible in your imagination of the meaning of that word in pink or **blue**.

Take **pont** (*bridge*), a feminine noun.
Imagine a Disneyland pink bridge, sparkling with light leading to a fairy castle with soldiers in pink uniforms lining up on either side
See it vividly in your imagination – **close your eyes and try it**!

Then forget it.

Like wearing arm-bands when you start swimming, once you get beyond a certain number of words this may not help. You could, however, establish the habit of learning a word in conjunction with one or more of the following methods.

2. Feminine nouns and **masculine nouns** respond differently to **Treiglad Meddal** and this creates another useful mnemonic device.

- When learning a new word, **learn it together with a mutatable adjective** cath fach (mutated) *kitten* as opposed to **ci bach** (non-mutated) *puppy*
- **Put 'y'** (*the*) **before the noun if it starts with a mutatable letter** 'y' gath fach (mutated) **'y' ci bach**

(non-mutated). Remember that 'll' and 'rh' are exceptions and do not mutate after '**y**'.

- **Put dau** (masculine) or **dwy** (feminine) **before the noun dau gi bach**, **dwy gath fach**. Remember that **dau**, although masculine, itself triggers Treiglad Meddal.

Nursery rhymes, popular songs and place-names can also be useful if they contain the appropriate mutation.

Dau gi bach yn mynd i'r coed.
Sosban fach yn berwi ar y tân.
Gafr wen, wen, wen [This is the mutated form of *gwen* which is the feminine form of *gwyn* ('white'). Don't worry about this for the time being.]
Graig Goch; Graig Wen, etc.

Afterword

The aim of this little book is to provide you with a basic tool-kit which you can use to repair sentences when things go wrong. Equally important, you need no longer be intimidated by more formal books of grammar; you know the terms and know how they function as you move on to learn and enjoy more of the language and its treasures.

You will also know by now how Welsh dictionaries work, and if you get stuck you could do worse than look at the more detailed work that I have undertaken in various dictionaries and books of grammar published by Gwasg Gomer, and on the website *Gweiadur.com*.